Shakespeare and Gende

CW00409046

Shakespeare in Practice

Series Editors:

Stuart Hampton-Reeves, Professor of Research-informed Teaching, University of Central Lancashire, UK, and Head of the British Shakespeare Association

Bridget Escolme, Reader in Drama and Head of the School of English and Drama, Queen Mary, University of London, UK

Published:

Shakespeare and Audience in Practice
Stephen Purcell

Shakespeare and Political Theatre in Practice
Andrew Hartley

Shakespeare and Gender in Practice
Terri Power

Forthcoming:

Shakespeare and Original Practices
Don Weingust

Shakespeare and Gesture in Practice
Darren Tunstall

Shakespeare and Space in Practice
Kathryn Prince

Shakespeare and Costume in Practice
Bridget Escolme

Shakespeare and Directing in Practice
Kevin Ewert

Shakespeare and Diaspora in Practice
Alexa Huang

Shakespeare and Digital Performance in Practice
Erin Sullivan

Shakespeare in Practice
Series standing order
ISBN 978–0230–27637–6 hardcover
ISBN 978–0230–27638–3 paperback
(*outside North America only*)

You can receive future titles in this series as they are published by placing a standing order. Please contact your bookseller or, in the case of difficulty, write to us at the address below with your name and address, the title of the series, and the ISBN quoted above.

Customer Services Department, Macmillan Distribution Ltd

Houndmills, Basingstoke, Hampshire, RG21 6XS, England

Shakespeare and Gender in Practice

Terri Power

 macmillan education   palgrave

First published 2016 by
PALGRAVE

Palgrave in the UK is an imprint of Macmillan Publishers Limited,
registered in England, company number 785998, of 4 Crinan Street,
London, N1 9XW.

Palgrave Macmillan in the US is a division of St Martin's Press LLC,
175 Fifth Avenue, New York, NY 10010.

Palgrave is a global imprint of the above companies and is represented
throughout the world.

Palgrave® and Macmillan® are registered trademarks in the United States,
the United Kingdom, Europe and other countries.

ISBN 978–1–137–40853–2 hardback
ISBN 978–1–137–40852–5 paperback

This book is printed on paper suitable for recycling and made from fully
managed and sustained forest sources. Logging, pulping and manufacturing
processes are expected to conform to the environmental regulations of the
country of origin.

A catalogue record for this book is available from the British Library.

A catalog record for this book is available from the Library of Congress.

Printed in China

Contents

Acknowledgements

This volume would not be possible without the outstanding contributions made by the artists and companies featured throughout. During my initial research period, I contacted many professional companies and artists in the US and UK and was humbled by all the contributing artists' interest and openness in participating in this study. I am especially grateful to artist, and feminist advocate, Lisa Wolpe, for graciously inviting me into her home and sharing her rich insights into performing beyond gender. I would also like to thank Joanne Zipay of the Judith Shakespeare Festival and Rebecca Patterson of the Queen's Company for their ongoing support of my research over the last decade. I am indebted to the brilliant dramaturg Lydia Garcia for sharing her research and experience working with the OSF company, and must also acknowledge the welcoming embrace I received from the team at OSF. Amy Richard was my angel, shepherding me about the facilities and arranging my schedule and interviews, and many thanks also go to the ladies in the basement archives that dusted off OSF cross-gender-performance articles and reviews for me. I would also like to thank Dugald Bruce-Lockhart for his candid and intelligent interview on Propeller and for sharing his insights on playing across genders in the productions of Propeller. I would also like to thank Chickspeare founder Sheila Snow Proctor for connecting with me in regard to the work that her company produces in North Carolina. I would also like to thank the brilliant and brave Roz Hopkinson for her continued support through the Stance Theatre Company.

This book would not be possible without the support of Bath Spa University and one of my biggest supporters, Mark Langley. Thanks also to Pamela Karatonis for her words of wisdom and suggestions. I also have to thank Peter Thomson and Christopher McCullough at the University of Exeter for their continued mentorship and knowledge. I also must thank the *Shakespeare in Practice* series editors Stuart Hampton-Reeves and Bridget Escolme for all their support and guidance in writing and publishing this work. I am so grateful to be part of the series and have the utmost respect for the project as a whole. Above all, I must thank my family: my wife Tammy for listening to me rattle on about Shakespeare and for travelling across two continents to collect interviews and attend performances; my grandmother Ruth Power for hosting and feeding me during the writing process; my mother for her unyielding belief in me; and my teenage sister Ruthanne for serving as my social media research assistant. I wish to dedicate this book to my two dads Peter Power and Clark Montgomery. They passed away during the research and writing period but were proud of my achievements. I am eternally grateful for all their support throughout my life.

Series Editors' Preface

The books in the *Shakespeare in Practice* series chart new directions for a performance approach to Shakespeare. They represent the diverse and exciting work being undertaken by a new generation of Shakespeareans who have either come to the field from theatre practice or have developed a career that combines academic work with performing, directing or dramaturgy. Many of these authors are based in Drama departments and use practical workshops for both teaching and research. They are conversant with the fields of English Literature and Performance Studies, and they move freely between them. This series gives them an opportunity to explore both fields and to give a greater prominence to some of the key questions that occupy performance studies in the study of Shakespeare.

We intend this series to shape the way in which Shakespeare in performance is taught and researched. Our authors approach performance as a creative practice and a work of art in its own right. We want to create a new curriculum for Shakespeare in performance, which embraces the full complexity of the art of theatre and is underpinned by performance theory.

The first part of each book explores the theoretical issues at stake, often drawing on key works in performance studies as well as seminal writings by theatre practitioners. The second part of the book consists of a series of critical studies of performance in practice, drawing on theatre history but chiefly focusing on contemporary productions and practitioners. Finally, we have asked all of our authors to engage in a debate with another scholar or practitioner so that each book ends with an engaging and unresolved debate.

All of our books draw on a wide range of plays so that teachers can choose which plays they want to focus on. There will be no volume on *Hamlet, A Midsummer Night's Dream* or *Romeo and Juliet* – every volume can be used as a model for every play in the canon. Similarly, none of the books exhaust the research possibilities that they open: there is more, much more, work to be done on every topic in this series.

Studies of Shakespeare in performance often leave aside the audience. Either the critic's own response is used to voice the audience, or the audience is effaced altogether. Questions about the role of the audience in constructing the theatrical event are often posed, but rarely answered, at conferences and seminars. Leaving the audience out of theatrical analysis is problematic, but including them is, if anything, even more problematic. How does one give voice to an audience? Is an audience exterior to the performance, or is it part of it – in which case, it is possible to 'read' the audience in a critical way? What research tools do we need to conduct such work? Or is the audience an illusion? Stephen Purcell addresses how notions of audience, audience configuration, audience expectation and audiences as they figure in play texts all produce meaning in the theatre. His work is the ideal book with which to begin this series.

The development of political theatre in the twentieth century has had a profound influence on the performance of Shakespeare's work. In a sense, Shakespeare's theatre has always been a political one which is keenly aware of its context. His earliest plays vividly dramatize the power games at the heart of England's bloody civil wars in the fifteenth century, and throughout his career, Shakespeare returned again and again to critical questions of authority, identity and transgression. This is one of the reasons why Bertolt Brecht studied the Elizabethan theatre, among other forms, when developing the "alienation" effect for his own highly politicized theatre. One of the consequences of Brecht's work, together with many other innovators from the last century, is that we can no longer approach Shakespeare performance in a neutral way. Andrew James Hartley's study is an important contribution to the series which demonstrates the potency (and the danger) of politicizing Shakespeare in performance.

The performance of gender in Shakespeare's plays has been a richly studied topic in Theatre studies, English literary studies and Early Modern scholarship. However, despite Shakespeare's diverse narrative profile of multiculturalism and his inclusive 'humanist' appeal, when it comes to gender in casting and playing, Shakespeare production often follows familiar, normative patterns. Terri Power's study of Shakespeare and gender challenges 'traditional' notions of casting and character through an intersectional feminist study of current Shakespeare in practice. The book explores questions of gender construction and performance arising from all-male 'original practices' productions of Shakespeare and all-female versions; challenges the stigma still attached to transvestism and cross-gender performance; offers new perspectives on how early modern attitudes to gender are dealt with in contemporary production; and considers broader issues around the terminologies, documentation and resources that might enable artists and scholars to archive and develop new challenges for Shakespeare audiences in the performance of gender.

Stuart Hampton-Reeves
Bridget Escolme

Introduction

'Shakespeare and his fellow actors... were not limited by the gender of the parts they played. They enjoyed a theatre of the imagination, where commoner played king, man played woman, and, within the plays, woman man. In Shakespeare, the disguise and revelation of everything, including gender, is central' (Rylance 2003). Actor Mark Rylance explains here that cross-gender performance was an integral part of Shakespeare's original theatrical practice. Despite London accounts from 'individuals who found the practice opprobrious' (Lublin 2012: 67) in society, Elizabethans enjoyed acts of cross-dressing on their stages and in their plays. Shakespeare, a shrewd businessman as well as playwright, capitalised on this interest by creating characters in his plays that are deeply entrenched in cultural gender prescriptions but find liberation from this dramaturgical gender bondage through acts of disguise and cross-gender playing. Doubly alluring for Elizabethan audiences was the cross-gender acting performed by the boy players in Shakespeare's company as they assumed the female roles in his plays.

Borrowing ideas from Judith Butler's gender performativity theory as expressed in *Gender Trouble* (1999), I aim to demonstrate that Shakespeare's theatre was, and is, embedded in acts of gender performance. In Part I, I will define the many acts encompassed by the term *cross-gender performance* and argue that gender, social and theatrical, are constructions and therefore performative through an intersectional feminist position. I will illustrate how we are programmed by society to 'do' gender and how we might also 'undo' gender so that it can be reproduced theatrically by differently sexed bodies, such as in the stylised femininity once presented in the performances of Shakespeare's boy players. Later, in the second part of the chapter, we will invert this practice to discuss how women playing male roles in Shakespeare's plays offers equality on our stages and liberates women from limitations placed upon them in our patriarchal society.

In Part II, we will survey the multitude of cross-gender approaches professional companies and actors are using to stage Shakespeare. We will look at similarities and differences in the practices of single-sex Shakespeare companies and productions, all-male and all-female. We will study how different creative casting approaches affect the

1

performative meanings in theatrical stagings of Shakespeare and look at how contemporary queer approaches to Shakespeare reveal evermore layers to gender performance theatrically as well as socially. Chapter 10 offers examples and exercises for you to explore performing cross-gender 'as you like it', and Part III with artist Lisa Wolpe concludes this volume, referencing some discussion points already presented and offering new insights as to how we might (re)dress Shakespeare in the future.

This study will focus on contemporary cross-gender approaches in practice in the UK and the USA. Currently these transatlantic theatrical companies are wrestling with issues regarding gender presentation and reflections of equality and diversity on our Shakespearean scaffold. It seems rather ironic to me that despite Shakespeare's diverse narrative profile of multiculturalism, univocal dialogue and inclusive 'humanist' appeal, Shakespeare as a theatrical genre is currently very conservative in casting and playing when compared to other classical forms such as dance and opera. There are exceptions and extraordinary examples of productions and companies in operation working to combat this limiting practice of 'traditionalist' Shakespeare, but the waves of change are regressed by a deeply held belief that there should be a Shakespeare 'tradition' and that tradition should be reflected in bodily form on our stages. In this volume, I aim to offer an alternative view of gender performance and dispel ideas about Shakespeare, its 'tradition' and notions of character through an intersectional feminist study of current Shakespeare in practice.

The cross-gender discussion will be furthered by introducing key debates in the field of Shakespeare and gender in performance. These debates will be framed with an analytical look at gender by applying gender theories to our review of key productions, performers and companies playing with gender as a trope in performance. Some of the practices we will encounter are self-referential, conservative and transparent. Others walk the line between normative and provocative, and a few are unabashedly *queer*.

Fear of the Feminine

Many gender scholars argue that gender is not a fixed category and its prescriptive language, norms and sets of behaviour vary culturally and across eras. Cross-dressing has historically engendered anxieties in many societies as it highlights the performative nature and fluidity of gender serving to destabilise social structures such as those found in Western patriarchal societies, and it also evokes deeply held anxieties towards the effeminisation of society and 'man' as a whole. This fear of the 'feminine' is pervasive throughout many cultures and eras and manifests itself in strongly held suspicions that theatre, the realm of cross-dressing and effeminised behaviour, thoughts and feelings, is a homosexual proving ground.[1]

This is clearly presented through scholarship in many studies on the topic of men and boy cross-dressing practices but such anxieties seem to be currently manifesting in the reverse, as women dress as men in contemporary Shakespearean productions. When women perform in roles traditionally played by male actors, they destabilise tightly held beliefs about male privilege, patriarchal positions of power, the performativity of masculinity and the subversive nature of cross-dressing once again. If, as puritan notions of cross-dressing assert, men and boys cross-dressing into female roles turns them 'into pansies' (Orgel 1996: xiv) then what happens to women in reverse? And why are women's cross-dressed performances deemed so threatening to our social order in this day and age? In fact, other eras embraced the convention as women were highly visible in cross-dressed roles, including portrayals of major Shakespearean male characters. So prevalent were these cross-gendered performances that it became fashionable to see a woman play in breeches for the erotic pleasure of seeing her ankles (Senelick 2000). However, this is routinely a lost and, sometimes, rediscovered history, normally neglected in studies on the topic, and it seems to me that there is a political function to 'forgetting' women's participation in these roles.

However, it is important for us to consider that Shakespeare's theatre has always been enlivened by the presence of women both on and off-stage, even in the Elizabethan era. Despite selective considerations of the contrary, women did perform and act on stages in England during the Elizabethan era. Stephen Orgel points out in *Impersonations* that women 'were a common place feature of the European stage' (1996: 1) during the Renaissance and in Shakespeare's England. Although European women were allowed to perform in plays of the period (even on stages across England), English actresses were mostly barred from performing publically because 'of the English equation of actresses with whores' (1996: 1). However, it is important to note that they were allowed to perform in private at Court and in Tudor pageants and masques, so long as they did so in 'amateur status' and not 'as a profession' (1996: 4). There are even a few notable exceptions in the research record including a 1611 solo performance at the Fortune by English actress Moll Frith who was the inspiration for the lead character in Middleton and Dekker's play *The Roaring Girl*.

This is a significant point considering that contemporary companies continue to use all-male castings and defend such exclusivity as a study in 'original practices'. The question arises; what original practices are these companies claiming and why return to a social standard that excludes women in a genre of work that already disenfranchises them? Is this practice a return to labelling female actors – actresses and therefore 'whores'? Are these male-focused practices attempting to, once again, preserve the 'sanctity of women' by barring them from the stage? It would seem to suggest so, as women performing as men in contemporary practice are overwhelmingly denigrated to 'amateur' status and are forced to perform in smaller less visible theatres with little to no funding. Women, particularly in cross-dressed roles, are given little to no access or status as 'professionals' whereas conversely, men establish cross-gender practice as a legitimate vocation through the label of 'original practices'.

Another issue faced by professionals working in this genre is the stigma attached to cross-gender performance. Our society likes to believe that gender is stable and insist that any whiff of transvestism in our theatre be transparent and non-threatening; if it takes fuller form and deceives us we become deeply disturbed. This is because we are programmed from an early age to believe that gender is fixed and aligned directly to one's sex; men are masculine and women feminine. Transvestism and cross-gender performance in theatre conflate this programming making us reconsider gender altogether. This can be a highly provocative and political act, as we will discover later in the book.

The Elizabethans saw gender as a biological binary made up of direct opposites and complements, and Shakespeare's theatre reflects this polarised view of gender and social politics of the time. However, it is important to note that gender is currently being argued by scholars and theorists as a condition that exists beyond biology, described as a social performance (Butler 1999, Bornstein 1994, West and Zimmerman 2009) or 'a quality to be striven for and maintained' (Orgel 1996: 19) such as in statements like 'be a man' and reprimands such as 'thy tears are womanish'. These statements and quotes have equivalents today as Orgel points out: 'There has always been a crucial behavioral element to gender that has nothing to do with the organs of generation' (1996: 19).

Gender in Shakespeare must always be a process of exploration and critique in order for it to hold meaning for our time. However, a conundrum arises as gender is still argued as fixed; patriarchal structures of power are still upheld, and the gender binary is at play often dominating our stages. Cross-gender practice is continually crippled by the stigma of modern aesthetics of realism and an emphasis on the bodies of actors rather than the art of acting. This is a dangerous prospect for Shakespeare practice as Shakespeare's theatre is one predicated upon the live but illusory world evoked by the play and the 'playing' and should not be bound to literal realities. In early modern Shakespeare performance, the gender of a character was rarely presented as a corpo-reality; the original players of Shakespeare were largely from lower to mercantile classes, not aristocracy, yet they played lords and kings on the Globe stage. They were predominately white Englishmen, yet some played Europeans and Moors. The boy players, and arguably male play-ers, assumed the roles of female characters – all within the context of theatrical 'playing', not realistic representations.

As an audience attending Shakespeare's plays, we are asked to imag-ine the setting on a bare scaffold, 'a kingdom for a stage' (*Henry V*, Act 1 Prologue), to imagine that the players are the characters they have been assigned, 'princes to act and Monarchs to behold', and the entire world of the play, 'make imaginary puissance ... for 'tis your thoughts that now must deck our kings'. Shakespeare's theatrical prac-tice demands a process that stretches our imagination (puissance) and requests that within that process we dress (deck) the players and 'piece out ... imperfections' (Prologue, 19–29) forgiving any contrary realities presented which should include the physical difference between actors and their roles.

Women and the Lost Tradition

Whilst conducting my research on all-female Shakespeare companies, I was surprised at the numbers of references to companies I found with little to no following information or documentation. For example, in an Internet search I found a brief article about the Women's Shakespeare Company and their all-female *Othello* (1999) performed in New York City.[2] The trail might have ended there, but I recognised a colleague's name in the credits and contacted her directly. She gave me pertinent information about the company and the production and even shared still photographs from the *Othello* performance. Had this moment of kismet not occurred, this work might have been forgotten, perhaps even lost forever.

This is the great conundrum of our discipline; it is richly alive, tem-poral and all too ephemeral. Almost as soon as we applaud our theatri-cal heroes, the curtain lowers and their efforts are lost in the sands of time. When we embark to uncover work from the past, we are seeking to answer some of the simplest of questions. Who were the significant players of Shakespeare? What did they do with the plays and their parts? Why has it been lost? In some cases, fragments are strewn about and can be reclaimed via the Internet, libraries and/or scholars of Shakespeare, but for the practice and performance of women and minority artists, this is all piecemeal.

Salvaging Shakespeare practice and performance history is a collective problem for many practitioners but a most pressing need for those at risk of losing their history to the tides of time. This book aims to document some of these stellar performances and practices, as they are being rediscovered, developed and preserved.

As I conducted research for this book, I soon discovered that, despite their recent engagement in theatrical history, little scholarship has been done on these particular areas of performance. In fact, there were very few books dedicated solely to the subject of women's and 'other' cross-gender performances. Most of the research I found included single papers, isolated chapters, scattered reviews and nearly non-accessible performance documentation. These resources were contained predominately within scholarship and documentation on men's cross-gender performances. It is my feeling that this area of performance, women's on-stage portrayal of masculinities, lacks documentation, scholarship and acknowledgement because it is doubly disadvantaged as both essentially a Queer area of study and of women's history.

This is not to say that there is no scholarship in the field that focuses on women's engagement in such cross-gender theatrical practices. Over the last decade there has been an increase of scholarship, study and even practice in this field, but many of these studies have served to document the performance histories (*Women as Hamlet* (2009)), to analyse the performances (*The Drag King Anthology* (2002) and *The Drag King Book* (1999)) or both (*The Changing Room* (2000)). Clearly missing from the field are practical accounts and studies of women performing masculinities as detailed by artists in practice. Not only are there few accounts with specific details of performances and practical processes, there is no thorough guide or focused discussion on the problems and pitfalls such performances and performers encounter. Such discussions and explorations of practice, from the perspective of the performer, are seriously neglected in this field and it seemed to me that addressing this shortcoming in the research record would be a necessary and revelatory endeavour. This is one reason this book focuses on women's and Queer performances of gender in contemporary Shakespeare practice and includes a workshop model.

The importance of such a perspective was made evident to me on 13 October 2008, when performance artist Claire Dowie[3] conducted a workshop with my nearly all-female Staging Shakespeare class held at Bath Spa University. Faced with the challenge of casting each other in mostly male roles for class assignments and having watched Dowie's transformative performance in her gender-bending production *From H to He (I'm Becoming a Man)*, the students questioned her approach to cross-gender practice. One student directly asked, 'How do you play a man?' Dowie found answering this question challenging as it was quite broad, but explained that she only played male characters she created in her work and 'wouldn't know how to play a man' in a naturalistic approach if she was 'given a script'. It was evident that my students were searching for practical answers – a guide to aid their own explorations as they wrestled with playing male Shakespeare roles in assignments.

I understand this conundrum faced by Dowie. It is very difficult to be a practitioner, scholar and teacher all at once. Dowie, as a solo performer and the sole creator of her works, doesn't have the luxury of time to stop mid-practice and analyse, record and disseminate her findings. The pressures of maintaining her professional status as a theatrical artist takes its toll and consumes much of her time: the rest of her time is spent artistically developing her work and, of course, living a private life. This conundrum is faced by the majority of professional artists I have interviewed and worked with over the last decade. They are developing their technique and testing ideas as part of their ongoing professional performance practice but rarely find the opportunity to reflect and document their discoveries for future work. This has resulted in a lack of analysis, documents and resources salvaging the working practices of artists in the field of cross-gender performance. This is another area of reclamation this volume seeks to address.

Terminology

There are many words and titles that will be under discussion throughout this book that need to be defined for clarification of use. Although some of these words and titles may be familiar to you, I want to point out how I am using them specifically to define a convention, idea or practice that is necessary for our study. The first terminology that pertains to our research that you will encounter throughout the volume is 'cross-gender performance'.

I use cross-gender performance as an umbrella term to indicate any performance of gender that crosses from one 'normative' gender performance to another. This performance of crossing usually assumes the reader understands gender in binary terms such as masculine and feminine, and the term signposts this act of crossing (from one gendered state to another) as a specific theatrical convention of performing the 'other' gendered state. Cross-gender performance includes even more specific theatrical gender performance conventions and acts, such as Drag, Drag Kings, boy players, female players, lady boys, otokoyaku, onnagatas, breeches roles and so on. My use of cross-gender as a term to indicate this particular crossing of gendered states in performance has been influenced by Rhonda Blair's chapter '"Not…But"/"Not-Not-Me": Musings on Cross-Gender Performance' in *Upstaging Big Daddy* (Donkin and Clement 1993). In this chapter, Blair does not define cross-gender performance but does an excellent job explaining the importance of 'crossing' in performance: 'The oscillations of identity an actor moves through in performing the other gender is in fact a process of finding that ostensible Other in the self'(1993: 291). Although most of the practice and research I discuss through the book fall under this term, I have discovered during the course of my research that it is limited, particularly as it assumes only two gendered states. This is why, I also employ the term 'trans-dressed performance'.

Trans-dressed performance or trans-dressing is used mostly in Chapter 9 and my use of these terms is influenced from transgender theory and Queer experiences of gender. In particular my perspective on this convention was inspired by Leslie Fienberg's *Transgender Warriors* (1996) and *Trans Liberation: Beyond Pink or Blue* (1998) and Kate Bornstein's *Gender Outlaw: On Men, Women and the Rest of Us* (1994). I use trans-dressed to define theatrical gender performances wherein actors not only 'cross' between genders but may cross back and forth, reside between or embody 'other' genders in a single performance. Trans-dressed performance includes alternative and unique explorations of gender identity and performance that are not possible in the definition of 'cross-gender performance' and its fixed assumption of two genders.

Other specific cross-gender performance conventions I discuss throughout the book will include Drag, Drag Kings and cross-dressed or cross-dressing in performance.

I use 'Drag' to mean camp and/or theatrical performances of gender that essentially are the hyper- and meta-theatrical performance of the socially prescribed performance of gender usually placed on stage to highlight the absurdity of rendering gender as 'natural' and/or to entertain and exercise Queer identities. Drag is a historically queer performance convention and its actors are both men and women: 'Drag

Queens' and 'Drag Kings' respectively. Drag Queens and Kings are usually noted as female and male impersonators, but I think that to call them impersonators is to once again limit the possibilities of these performance conventions. It is my experience that both Drag Queens and Kings do much more than just 'impersonate' female and male figures in their performance acts and the term impersonation, when discussing gender performance, becomes problematic as it is argued by several feminist scholars including Simone de Beauvoir [4] that women perform their femininity through acts of impersonation.[5] Here, the defining of Drag as an impersonation becomes complicated as it is theorised that gender (masculine and feminine) is a socially prescribed impersonation performed every day. In this view, there can be no distinction between Drag and this impersonation of gender for social distinction between the sexes. For this reason and to keep this distinction clear, I do not refer to Drag Queens or Kings as impersonators. They may at times impersonate an iconic figure, but their acts are much more than 'impersonations' of gender and my use of the term throughout this book serves to acknowledge this understanding.

One of the more confusing terms used may be 'cross-dressed performance'. The term has been used to describe cross-gender performances in theatre and usually references a history of cross-dressing both on stage and offstage. Cross-dressing shares roots with transvestism but as a theatrical convention cross-dressing is less a social identity than transvestism (although theatrical cross-dressers may be transvestites or borrow from transvestism and its aesthetics) and more a performance of the opposite gender. My use of cross-dressed performance as a term seeks to describe a theatrical practice wherein cross-gender performances are meant to be received as naturalistic. In cross-dressed performance the audience is asked to 'suspend disbelief' and to accept that the gender of the character is 'stable' and usually heteronormative. Cross-dressed performance does not reference the actor's gender or biological sex in the performance, as one might encounter in Drag performances.

Throughout the book, my use of dramatic language such as 'acts', 'perform', 'audience' and 'performer' will at times double in meaning. Some of these theatrical words will be crafted to also reference terminology used by gender theorists such as Judith Butler. They have borrowed from theatrical and dramatic terminology in order to highlight their theories of gender and its 'performativity'. Their appropriation of theatrical language reinforces the idea that gender is not a state of 'being' but an action, a doing, and a doing that is not for oneself but for an assumed audience and therefore is a social, political and dramatic act.

This study constantly negotiates between social and theatrical gender performativity in order to critique gender performance altogether. By deconstructing and (re)constructing gender in theatrical performance, social gender performativity and its codified structure and restrictions are dramatically staged. Gender becomes a site of interrogation and play, a place for new performance expressions (social and artistic) that defines itself with and against real or imagined bodies.

Feminist Theory and Shakespeare

To many in the Western world the project of feminism is over, anti-quated or stigmatised. Feminist theory has splintered to create other feminisms and the analysis has been fraught with internal as well as external tensions and critiques. Feminist movements, also referred to as waves, have given rise to current manifestations of intersectional-feminist, post-feminist, cyber- and techno-feminist thinking and theory. The real question is why apply a feminist analysis now, and to the study and practice of Shakespeare? Primarily because the project of feminism is not over, particularly in relation to the study and prac-tice of Shakespeare, as this volume will demonstrate. Throughout this book, I will present a feminist analysis and practice of gender drawing upon early and contemporary feminist and Queer studies with an emphasis on gender performativity theory as introduced by Judith Butler, intersectional-feminist paradigms and transgender – Queer feminist analysis in an attempt to offer a critique of gender that includes otherness, as 'second', multiple sexes and unique genders emerge in our theatres.

Is Simone de Beauvoir right when she states that 'when man makes of woman the *Other*' the woman 'may fail to lay claim to the status of subject because she lacks definite resources' and is 'very well pleased with her role as the *Other*'? (1997: 21). This statement is suspect as subjectivity is under question. When we read history, whose history is being recounted? Who selects this history for recording above others? De Beauvoir goes on to quote feminist philosopher Poulain de la Barre: 'All that has been written about women by men should be suspect, for the men are at once judge and party to the lawsuit'(1997: 21).

Shakespeare's work needs to be suspect as well. Many scholars have unearthed how Shakespeare comments on expectations of gender in Elizabethan England. Good English virtues and Christian morals are also embedded deeply in his works. So how does the same writer gain global, humanist and even timeless titles? Colin Chambers in his book *Inside the Royal Shakespeare Company* explains:

> No other artist carries the historical and global baggage that Shakespeare does and, equally, no other offers the limitless opportunities for artistic exploitation. (Chambers 2004: 115)

It is the baggage, reputation, kudos and artistic exploration that have drawn many to study and perform Shakespeare, even forming entire companies such as the Royal Shakespeare Company (RSC), Shakespeare's Globe Theatre (SGT), The Original Shakespeare Company and the Oregon Shakespeare Festival based upon his canon. Many of these companies, like Chambers' RSC study reveals, have to defend their artistic expression against the 'myth' of Shakespeare as it generates traditionalist and mostly conservative expectations, usually involving lots of men on stage wearing doublets and hose.

> Despite sustained attacks, 'Shakespeare' has retained his special place in British and world culture: 'Shakespeare' has remained national and international, particular and universal, esoteric and transcendental – the globalising myth, in which everyone's history seems to be written, the more so as his own biography is very thin. Without the popularity of 'Shakespeare' there would have been no RSC in the first place. And while the RSC would never challenge the heart of the myth – the unparalleled greatness of the plays – there has been a struggle in riding the myth to balance authority with innovation, to use the myth rather than be used by it. (2004: 116)

This is the tightrope walked by many Shakespeare companies, and pressures to uphold the myth are forcing companies to rethink their performance approach and programming of the plays. The current fashion to see Shakespeare in historical dress, and in far more myth-invoking productions than in the past, seems counter-intuitive to our developing social liberation, inclusive cultures and technological advances that persuade us all to be free, open and connected global communities. Perhaps it is simply a conservative backlash from the number of postwar modern-dress productions that dominated the twentieth century throughout Europe and the Americas.

Whatever the reason such conservative tastes have emerged, I agree with Chambers that the remedy lies in the interpretation, adaptation, casting and acting approaches towards the work in performance. An examination of approaches taken to stage the final act of *The Taming of the Shrew* is a good example. The play has historically been such a problem for feminists and contemporary audiences that it is often 'reimagined' by companies, making it a key play for feminist critique and debate.

The play's narrative focuses on a battle of wills between the 'Shrewish' Kate and her 'manly' suitor (later husband) Petruchio. The play can be seen as a manifestation of the battle of the sexes, and a blueprint for Elizabethan and, possibly, current prescriptive social gender roles. Feminist scholars have been divided on the overall interpretation of the play and the reading of Kate's 'taming' as expressed in her last speech, arguing that it is either an 'animal-like' result of Petruchio's abusive 'taming tactics' (Bean 1983: 66) or an indication that she is only tamed through her own free will and ability to love the man she is forced to wed.

These interpretations through feminist critique have been theatrically manifested in contemporary performances of *The Taming of the Shrew* around the globe. For example, the 2009 RSC production of *The Taming of the Shrew* starring Michelle Gomez, as Kate, presented the play's grim misogyny in stark contrast to other family-friendly, comic interpretations staged at the time. There was no withholding on the physical, emotional and psychological abuse of the character at the hands of her husband and other male characters in the play. Towards the end of the play, the audience watched in horror as she lifted up her skirt, bowing over a table, and offering herself to Grumio as part of her submission. Charles Spencer of *The Telegraph* (2009) stated that the director, Conall Morrison, 'pays Shakespeare the compliment of presenting the play that he actually wrote' and seemed disturbed by the savage cruelty. The audience may also have found the production difficult to watch as the comedic playing and traditionally humorous moments in the play were 'greeted by stony audience silence, and there is something deeply unattractive about watching a woman being abused for three hours'.

However, there have also been dozens of companies that have tackled the blatant misogynistic undertones with clear feminist sympathies by reimaging and editing the text, creatively directing and casting the play or emphasising the farcical commedia influences to distance the 'taming' from any sense of realism. For example, Edward Hall's all-male company Propeller has been touring their version of *The Taming of the Shrew* since 2006 and presents an interpretation that gives Kate, played by Dan Wheeler, far more moxie than was presented by Gomez in the RSC's 2009 production. In keeping with Propeller's emphasis on highly physical playing and use of architectural space, Kate bounds across the stage, even leaping out of Petruchio's (Dugald Bruce-Lockhart) grasp onto the top of a giant wardrobe (about six feet off the ground), and her ability to throw crushing blows with her fists is evidenced. This is a Kate that can give as good as she gets. Her final submission speech is far more heartfelt and spirited than the forced 'zombified' declaration given by Gomez. This is a hard-hitting feminist interpretation presented, interestingly, by an all-male company.

Although the project of feminism may seem over, generally in our society, women have found *near* equal status. She receives 80% salary in comparison to men's and 30% representation in politics and upper management positions despite making up 52% of the population, and being overqualified for many of the professional positions she secures, for the most part, she is equal. No longer is she shackled to her biology. She can control her fertility as she has access to birth control. She no longer gets sold off into sexual slavery or is forced to marry a man of her father's choosing.

Today's women no longer are subjected to clitoral mutilation, female castration or religious and psychological torments in order to 'keep them in their place' (de Beauvoir 1997: 23). There are no longer scientific studies proving that women are inferior to men because her brain is smaller or religious doctrines dictating that she is sinful, evil, soiled and solely responsible for the fall of man – in need of punishment for simply being born a woman. These statements might ring true for women in Western culture, but the sad reality is that they are not true for women in other corners of the globe. Shakespeare's Globe presented the world through cross-gender performance, and our productions of Shakespeare should reflect the diverse profile of our society through male, female and other cross-gender practices. The feminist battle is not over, not won at all but still raging – on and off our stages.

Part I
In Theory

1
Gender Theory

In terms of my discussion of cross-gender performance as applied to Shakespeare, it needs to be rooted in an analytical framework that can help to unpack cultural notions of gender and gender-biased assumptions, identify the policing agents of gender and prescriptive ideologies, deconstruct articulations of gender in terms of social and theatrical acts and investigate reconstructions on differently configured bodies and in non-normative play in front of audiences. In order to facilitate such a discussion I have turned to key gender theorists, beginning with feminist theories, such as introduced by early feminist scholars (de Beauvoir, Dworkin and West) and newer, arguably also queer and liberal, stances made by Butler, Halberstam and Bornstein.

My reasoning for applying these theoretical viewpoints to this study of cross-gender Shakespeare in contemporary performance was that initially it was the early feminists that introduced considerations of gender, of women, as a category for study and focus, recognising patriarchal privilege and identifying the state of 'otherness' in a male-dominated culture. Feminists, and later Queer scholars, began to identify 'gender' and acknowledge genders in a plural sense (plurality), highlighting that there were more states of 'beingness'[1] than being male.

These scholars have investigated all aspects of gender in terms of social, psychological, ontological and political construction. All of these areas of study are highly important to any discussion and understanding of gender but far too vast for me to cover in this volume. However, I will be drawing upon key foundational concepts to illuminate areas of my study such as in discussing the cultural expectations of gender in contemporary Western society, exclusively the USA and UK. By teasing out these expectations through a feminist viewpoint I hope to create a shared analytical framework for discussing, deconstructing, reconsidering and playing with gender in theatrical practice.

Introducing feminist theory

Feminist theories and actions have historically faced internal and external challenges including conflicting messages and definitions of purpose and values. Early feminist Rebecca West (1913) stated

> 'I myself have never been able to find out precisely what feminism is: I only know that people call me a feminist whenever I express sentiments that differentiate me from a doormat or a prostitute.'

Although it is a highly referenced point in women's history, the feminist project known as the Women's Movement began much earlier than the explosive 1960s, growing in response to the work of early feminists like West, and female literary figures such as Schreiner, Woolf, de Beauvoir (Barry 1995: 121) and early liberationists that achieved voting and educational rights for women. Among its many aims, and pertinent to later discussions in this volume, the movement emphasised a critique of the Western canon in order to analyse women's representation in the works, questioning their invisibility as primary subjects and authors. A great deal of writing from this wave of feminist thinking and theory focused on deconstructing classical texts and revisioning new possibilities for interpretation and representation that actively empowered women, rather than passively ignoring them. Feminists also spent time uncovering classical female writers and placing them at the forefront of scholarship and critical inquiry. A move to reconcile 'his' story with 'her' story was enacted as 1970s feminists 'switched to the need to construct a new canon of women's writing by rewriting the history of the novel and poetry in such a way that neglected women writers were given new prominence' (1995: 122–3). Current feminist criticism, scholarship and politics are direct descendants, 'a product of the "women's movement" of the 1960s' (1995: 121), and continue to consider how women's representation in literature and media supports a liberated role for women or serves to derail her hard-fought independence. However, since the 1960s feminist theory and criticism have been influenced by other theories: poststructural, postmodern, Marxism, and so on, and therefore when we refer to feminist theory we must think in plurality, as there is no longer one feminist position but many. Although they may share 'woman' as a principle subject, men have also contributed to feminist thinking and politics and even become a subject of concern as well.

Involving men in feminist dialogue has been a contentious issue across the different waves of feminist critique. Radical feminists (Dworkin, Firestone and Solanas) were the most disagreeable, forming women-only projects and spaces and working tirelessly to undo patriarchal programming and to develop new social, political, stylistic and even linguistic models of behaviour and communication (Crow 2000), all in the absence of men. Conversely, liberal feminisms, including Queer and intersectional feminisms, hold many of the same aims as early feminists but include men in their scope of study, mandating that equality is a project for all of society and therefore should include people of differing sexes, sexualities, races, religions and varying economic and social statuses.

My position, as evidenced throughout this volume, is of a liberal feminist position. In the past I have worked and lived in women-only contexts, projects and communities and certainly can see benefits from such endeavours. I recognise that I owe a great deal to my radical and liberal feminist sisters, in terms of my continued recognition of how I am affected by our patriarchal political and social structure and understanding of how single-sex environments can be important tools for exploring and discussing gender or gender bonding in the absence of 'men' or external 'other'. I will explore this point fully in the discussion of Phylida Lloyd's all-female *Julius Caesar* (2012) and we will hear from a few artists interviewed in this volume who find great value working in single-sex companies and projects.

However, I believe the fundamental issue of equality requires a great deal of education, action, diversity of experience and communal focus, and leaving men, or any group, out of that dialogue will not help us achieve our ends. Our collective actions must eradicate inequality by dismantling the political structure that creates oppression of others both internally as well as externally.

Social gender programming: Is gender essential or performed?

Describing the performative aspects of gender drag artist RuPaul in his memoir Lettin It All Hang Out (1996) explained to readers that simply

'We're born naked, and the rest is drag.'

One of the primary contemporary debates about gender is whether it is an essential condition based on biology or a constructed one dictated by culture. Judith Butler tackles this question in *Gender Trouble* (1999), aligning her argument with early feminist thinking whilst taking new directions to conclude that gender is socially constructed and that governing 'gender laws' is 'inscribed on anatomically differentiated bodies' (1999: 12). She also questions the mechanism of gender construction (1999: 11) and explains that the essentialist position is mistakenly not based on biology:

> When the relevant 'culture' that 'constructs' gender is understood in terms of such a law or sets of laws, then it seems that gender is as determined and fixed as it was under the biology-is-destiny formulation. In such a case, not biology, but culture, becomes destiny. (1999: 12)

Feminist projects set about 'undoing' such gender constructs, freeing individuals from repressive and prescriptive categorisation. In order to address notions of equality and diversity in society, it becomes a task for us to rethink how we 'essentialise'/'do' gender culturally and work to 'undo' the laws, dispelling cultural myths about men and women, masculinity and femininity, and gender binary thinking altogether.

In order to achieve this 'undoing' as a practical approach, particularly as applied to the performance of Shakespeare, we must first investigate what the gender laws are in our culture, identify its hallmarks and semiotics and recognise how we participate in the everyday performance of gender. We start our study with an interrogation of our social performance of gender in order to understand how we might 'hold the mirror up to nature' and distort her picture on the 'unworthy scaffold'. Once we identify and define the ways in which we are 'gendered', how we perform our gender as a social construct, we can pervert these laws in subversive ways and undo the power of gender programming at the source – culture.

Doing gender

In contemporary Western society the social gendering process 'begins the moment we are born; with a simple question; is it a boy or a girl; and each of the agencies of socialization reinforces the gender stereotypes' (Emolu 2014: 23). Babies are immediately anatomically identified by their sexual parts and distinguished as boys or girls or male or female.

> There's a real simple way to look at gender: Once upon a time, someone drew a line in the sands of a culture and proclaimed with great self-importance, 'On this side, you are a man; on the other side, you

are a woman.' It's time for the winds of change to blow that line away. Simple. (Bornstein 1994)

The inherent problem with this gendering process is that children are being sexually categorised and placed in a binary formulation wherein males gain immediate power and privilege. Elizabeth P. Rahilly (2014: 4) explains, 'The first question that is asked after a child is born is the first of many iterations of this belief system, around which myriad institutions and practices are arranged.' This process does not recognise the fact that biologically there are other sexes, such as hermaphrodites that are born into this 'system' where there is, upon birth, no place for them (Feinberg 1996). Countless families are faced with this conundrum and have to make the harrowing decision to surgically turn their newborn into a male or female child. All too many times these decisions are completely irrevocable and destroy lives.

Once anatomically categorised, also known as 'biologically determining gender',[2] getting the babies to conform to the gender laws becomes the task of the parents, family and friends. 'In these ways, the gender binary functions as a "truth regime"[3] in society' (Rahilly: 4). Colour, for example, is used in infancy so as to codify sexual difference; boys are given blue tones and girls pink. Parents initially feel compelled to gender their children in keeping with binary prescriptive laws:

> The 'truth regime' framework intersects with the 'doing gender' approach. The dictates of the gender truth regime powerfully inform inter-actional practices, to which parents at first feel accountable. (5)

These colour codes signal to strangers the sex of the baby at a time when children look most similar as they have not begun to physically change biologically or learned to perform their gender as prescribed. This gender codifying of babies allows everyone to take part in the gendering process of the child before the child recognises an independent self.

This process continues to be forcibly mandated by family, peers, educators and the media as children 'are socialized into their gender roles and are taught what it means to be male or female' (Emolu 2014: 23). Interesting studies have been done on this subject, including the effects of consumerism and gender-typing on children (Freeman 2007) looking how 'gender appropriate' toys given to children establish their future gender roles and even employment possibilities: 'their toy choices have also been shown to have long term consequences for later social and cognitive development' (Cherney *et al* 2003: 96).

For example, girls are routinely given toys that 'elicit nurturing, proximity and role play' (96) preparing young girls for domestic life and child-rearing. Boys are given constructive toys that emphasise building and 'foster higher mobility, activity and manipulative play' (97) preparing them for industrial and scientific professions.[4] Moreover, girls' toys are defined as 'feminine' and given such qualities as 'attractive, creative, nurturing and manipulable' (97). These feminine toys often stimulate fantasy and highly vivid imaginations in young girls, whereas the masculine toys given to boys such as 'balls, guns and construction toys' are described as 'more competitive, aggressive, constructive' and 'reality based' (97).

Such distinction has meant that young people are gender stereotyped from birth and individual expression in both male and female children is often repressed. This is a crippling system for both men and women. For example, although men may receive the power and privilege over women in our society, it comes at a personal cost. Many men have reported that they were raised to not show affection and learned to suppress inner feelings. Seidler (1989) explains that masculinity is 'identified with rationality' and his experience of being a man in society meant that Seidler lost 'a sense of individual identity' and that 'learning to be a man means learning to be impersonal' (113). Like Seidler, many men struggle to maintain intimate relationships later in their adult lives and admit that they were not encouraged or taught to nurture children and others in the way women were in their formative years. The result of such gender socialising is that many men feel they have no connection to an interior self and 'barely get a chance to value a connection' to their 'inner lives' (116) as well as their personal needs. Many men, as boys, are taught that 'emotions are unseemly' and this causes breakdowns in their later intimate relationships and marriages as they struggle to share their feelings with their partners; 'though women have been rendered invisible in history and the public realm, men have been rendered invisible to themselves' (122).

These issues propelled 'the Men's Movement' making masculinity and men an area of enquiry and focus in the 1980s and 1990s. The work of the Women's Movement and feminist critique and practice inspired liberal-minded men to reclaim their lives and break free of the gender laws through male/masculinity consciousness raising. Men created spaces for sharing intimate thoughts and feelings with others and aimed to embrace their 'feminine' attributes, rather than 'despise our softer feelings' choosing to 'recognize them as integral parts of ourselves' (195).

Men began to break away from stereotypical roles, taking employment in traditionally female professions and roles such as nursing, child-rearing and homemaking.

In terms of our discussion of gender performativity and the 'doing' of gender, masculinity can be defined as the polar opposite performance of gender from that of femininity. In our male-centric society masculinity is seen as the one 'true' gender' (the rest are 'other' or non-genders) and establishes its dominance as natural through appropriation of mostly unnatural signs. Through closer observation, these 'natural' character-istics are found to be infinite in expression as no two masculinities are alike and become increasingly diverse across cultures and generations. However, 'gendering' processes (under a patriarchal ideology and politi-cal system that creates a gender binary and is predicated upon its stabil-ity) categorise and value these characteristics as authentic, biological and desirable.

These culturally constructed categories function as generic prescrip-tions for gendered behaviour and social coding, resulting in gender stereotypes. The effect is that all bodies and physical expressions are read as gendered; humans are 'not legible until gendered' (Butler (1999) and put into categories of male/masculine and female/feminine. This hetero-sexist patriarchal conditioning, starting at birth, mandates that we enact these designated stereotypes through physical and material signs conveying gender semiotic language that is legible, constant and repeatable. The social gendering system seeks to persuade us that gender is an essential biological condition that is entirely 'natural'. Throughout this volume we will interrogate this idea by exploring the myriad of ways we can play and perform gender through the works and characters of Shakespeare.

Heteronormativity

Another adverse effect of the social gendering process is not only the repression of unique identities and personal expression, as illustrated in the previous discussion, but also mandated conformity to heter-onormativity. Heteronormativity can be defined as a social set of acts and behaviours designed to constitute and regulate 'bodies according to normative notions of sex, gender and sexuality' (Lloyd 2013: 818). Linked closely to gender socialisation, heteronormativity insists that biological sex, gender expression and sexual preference are congru-ent and therefore natural; men are masculine and attracted to women.

Heteronormativity asserts that people are naturally heteronormative in sex and gender presentation, as well as heterosexual, and does little to recognise any alternatives to this assertion: 'heteronormative assumptions are those that view heterosexuality as natural, inevitable, and desirable' and use such assumptions to justify heterosexual privilege (Montgomery and Stewart 2012: 164).

With the rise of the gay liberation movement in the 1960s, homosexuality and alternative genders became visible and began to challenge the supremacy of heterosexual privilege and heteronormativity's 'natural' claim, biological essentialism. Gay, Queer and transgender scholars interrogated heteronormativity and activists sought to change perceptions and resist its stranglehold. Younger and some older generations have shifted such perceptions and now more easily accept sexual difference; current homosexuality and gender studies reveal that 'Attitudes toward gay rights and same-sex marriage have become more positive in the past few decades' (164). However, heteronormativity still is a system of privilege and power that is pervasive over the lives of many, particularly people that fall between or outside of the binary hetero-matrix.

Heteronormativity, as applied to some, can be a violent policing of gender expression, such as in the killing of transwoman Gwen Araujo in 2002. Although this case demonstrates extreme violence, in Araujo's case resulting in death, heteronormativity places many interlopers on dangerous ground. As Moya Lloyd (2013) points out, there are a large number of grim reminders of this policing as evidenced on the 'Transgender Day of Remembrance' website. And it is not just transgendered persons that are violently targeted. Homophobic hate crimes are also heavily documented, and many of us are victims of such 'street policing' in our society.

For example, my wife who identifies her gender as 'masculine' is a teacher in a private school and wears 'male'-identified clothing as she teaches. One day her class of six- and seven-year olds discussed the topic stating that it was 'okay for girls to wear boy's clothes' but that it was 'illegal for boys to wear girls' clothes'. When she tried to correct them on the issue, even explaining that she knew lots of 'men who dress as women', they still insisted that it was against the law. This was 2015 in a very liberal school in Southern California. My wife found this statement perplexing, explaining to me that she knew that the parents of her children would never have had such a conversation with their children or supported this idea. So where, she wondered, had such a thought been introduced?

This is the invisible violence of heteronormativity as discussed by Lloyd:

> Attention must also be paid, however, to the multiple modalities through which heteronormativity performs its violence on, through, and against bodies and persons. This includes but is not limited to the violence of gender norms; the way those norms work to position certain bodies and persons outside the realm of 'recognizable' violence. (2013: 820)

That children are predisposed to notions of gender heteronormativity at such an early age and with such strict notions of regulation as it being 'illegal' seems a violent and repressive assault on the developing psyche of these young people.

Prescriptive limitations of heteronormativity also affect performers who cross-dress on our stages, directors who wish to play with such norms and audiences' response to non-normative castings and gender play in contemporary productions of Shakespeare. Cross-gender Shakespeare as a practice is an important tool for challenging cultural gender stereotypes and for staging 'otherness'. All of the productions and companies and artists featured in this volume are appropriating, dismantling, challenging and redressing Shakespeare in engaging and provocative stagings and making inroads in changing attitudes and perceptions of gender. We are asked as an audience to rethink gender and reimagine Shakespeare. In turn, we also begin to redress ourselves and reimagine the world around us as we are presented with gender alternatives to those presented on a 'traditional', and all too often, repressive stage.

2
Actor–Audience Dynamics at Play in Gender Performance

One major consideration, often overlooked in performance explorations of gender is the importance of the audience in the interactive event of 'gendering' a performer. Butler describes this in *Gender Trouble* (1999) explaining that gender is defined and performed through repetitive acts of social interaction and intelligibility. These acts do not exist in a vacuum but rather in constant consort with an external audience, for one does not perform gender acts for oneself but for an audience that dictates and recognises those acts and therefore interprets the performance in order to gender the performer.

When a performer on stage highlights the theatrical and social semiotics of gender, particularly in cross- and trans-gender play, their act doubles not only as a heteronormative (re)presentation but also as a social and political critique of that representation, marking the performance as 'queer' in context. Jill Dolan in *Presence and Desire* writes, 'To be queer is not who you are, it's what you do, it's your relation to dominant power, and your relation to marginality, as a place of empowerment' (1999: 5). Cross-gender performance, in all of its many forms, presents Queer positions, viewpoints, attitudes and styles regardless if such effects were intended or not. It creates a particular relationship with the audience, an audience that has expectations of gender, gender roles and cultural rules for 'performing' gender through acts, styles and articulations. The audience cannot help but participate in applying their expectations to the performance and this serves to disrupt or enliven their theatrical experience.

It is important to consider that both gender performance and theatre are embedded in 'Queer' acts of deconstruction, discord and the subversion of dominant ideologies:

> Theatre and queer theory challenge ideas of fixed identities. Both break through the seemingly impermeable walls of gender and sexual categories by unmooring them from the idea that they derive absolutely and inevitably from an original objective source. (Solomon and Minwalla 2002: 14)

This is not to say that governing ideologies have no value in Queer explorations of gender performance and theory. The social 'everyday' performance of gender and its ontological material effects, language, codes and acts are blueprints for the 'extra-daily'[1] performance of gender on the stage. I reason that if the audience in the theatre is the same audience that 'genders' the actor on the street outside the theatre, this audience will also use the same gendering process and language to gender the character the actor plays on the stage. Therefore it is imperative, particularly in cross- and trans-gender castings, that the actor not only understands this process and its codes, but also employs practices that help build the character's gender in consort with or against the social and political gender ideology of the actor's 'theatrical' audience.

This performance of socialised ideologies of gender construction is discussed further and set against theatrical language and modes of presentation by Elin Diamond in *The Drama Review*:

> Gender refers to the words, gestures, appearances, ideas and behavior that dominant culture understands as indices of feminine or masculine identity. When spectators 'see' gender they are seeing (and reproducing) the cultural signs of gender and by implication, the gender ideology of a culture. Gender, in fact provides a perfect illustration of ideology at work since 'feminine' or 'masculine' behavior usually appears to be a natural – and thus fixed and unalterable – extension of biological sex. (1988: 84)

Understanding the gendering process, codes, rules and parameters is a fundamental, and often overlooked, aspect to cross-gender performance. When a performer understands such processes they may reproduce, disrupt or interrogate them with artistic and political impact. Such negotiations of understanding, decoding, exploring and parsing of normative gender prescriptions can prove enlightening to actors and audiences, making us all acutely aware of the confining limits 'gendering' people place on our collective progress.

3
ShakesQueer

As discussed earlier, from feminist theory also came subsets of critical studies that included a focus on further subjects, rather than a focus primarily on women. Queer theory, for example, emerged from this discourse and drew upon key feminist principles whilst also marking fertile soil to bear its own fruits. Queer theoretical perspectives are essential to a discussion of gender performance and social politics because theatre and cross-gender performance are inherently queer and Queer studies offer a critical lens that looks beyond prescriptive categories, and influences active, rather than passive, analysis. Like gender performance, Queer is a 'doing', a process by which subjects question and challenge prescriptive definitions and social labelling. Queer subjects, men, women 'and the rest of us' (Bornstein 1994) draw upon their personal experience – much like the feminist 'personal is political' mantra – and share their viewpoint of social processes that have failed them, that they have stepped away from or with which they are in a constant state of war. Their 'crisis' with binary gender laws and demands of heteronormativity places them in command position to challenge hetero-patriarchal uniformity and to do so through their own queer processes, rejecting gender stereotypes, traditional methods and prescriptive social roles and rules.

For our study, queering Shakespeare serves as a tool for rediscovering Shakespeare's characters and the act of performing gender for audiences. As a process, queering allows us to step into and then far away from gender stereotypes and social roles, giving actors more freedom to express new models of working on character with far more freedom to play with gender in construction and performance. If queering aids in our ability to revision characters and gender typing altogether, then it also serves to give us the freedom to reimagine ourselves and the extensive possibilities for our lives – free of the gender jailhouse.

In order to approach a practical research investigation, the best theoretical model we can explore in practice is outlined in Judith Butler's book *Gender Trouble* (1999) and her study of 'gender performativity'. Butler's work, like my own, is recognisably Queer, feminist and written through a lesbian viewpoint. Butler's theoretical/political influences are clearly evident throughout this key text, and she makes distinct statements to assert her points from this unique subject position. Some of her key arguments include her declaration that there is a social sexual hierarchy that 'produces and consolidates gender' (1999: xii) and that this is a crucial problem to individuals and identity. Further arguments are made regarding 'phallogocentrism' and the 'appropriation and suppression of the Other' (1999: 19) and the lesbian gender dilemma wherein Butler claims that 'lesbian appears to be a third gender or, as I shall show, a category that radically problematizes both sex and gender as stable political categories of description' (1999: 14). Such points are valuable to our understanding of gender performativity in theory and practice and further detail how queer identities and positions serve to unseat heteronormative dominance.

Butler's theory also acts as a springboard for our discussion due to the particular theoretical descriptions that Butler uses to illustrate her points. Throughout *Gender Trouble*, Butler expresses that gender is a process of 'doing' and 'proves to be performative' (1999: 33) and uses theatrical language throughout her book to further illustrate this crucial point. Gender performativity is a primary focus of this study, and by seeking to explore gender through an analysis of gender performance, social and theatrical, and through examination of practical examples set by others, we discover how gender can be done and undone in performances of Shakespeare's plays.

In addition to using Butler's gender performativity theory as a foundation for this study, I also want to introduce important Queer theoretical writings that are also relevant to an analysis of gender in practice and performance, particularly the work of another Judith, Judith Halberstam. Halberstam is an interesting and current figure in the field of gender and performance studies. Her work in the late 1990s was uniquely placed within the Drag King community and her descriptions, analysis and archive of this modern cross-gender convention benefitted many later studies of cross-gender performance. Halberstam also furthered her understanding and articulation of the female cross-gender convention through the publication of books and papers that placed the convention in Queer context and began a study of transgender theory and its relation to Drag, Drag Kings and art.[1]

Halberstam's later studies are heavily moored in transgender theory, and it was this introduction and the interesting arguments she presents on the topic in *Female Masculinity* (1998) and *In a Queer Time and Place: Transgender Bodies, Subcultural Lives* (2005) that drew me towards a study of transgender theory in performance and its applications in practical explorations. My interest in transgender discourse is rooted in my own personal experience of social and 'theatrical' gender performance. I identify with genderqueers as I have swapped genders on the binary in my social performance of gender throughout my life and routinely challenged gender 'norms' through cross-gender casting on stage:

> People who are *genderqueer* do not identify within the male/female binary, and instead may identify as being neither woman or man, or a little bit of both, or as being gender-fluid (i.e., moving between different gendered states over the course of their lives). (Serano 2013: 19)

I also appreciate transgender considerations placed on the importance of self-identity and the recognition of lived experiences of gender, rather than biologically defined when born. I personally experienced such considerations when my transgendered childhood friend fought vehemently to be recognised as 'his' proper sex and medically and psychologically changed from 'her' to 'him'. This experience was the basis for writing my play *Drag King Richard III* discussed in detail in the 'Queer Shakespeare' chapter. Having lived so closely to a transsexual (FTM)[2] through the process of transitioning allowed me to recognise that experiences of gender are not to be loosely categorised or easily dismissed; gender can be, for some, the nexus of identity and 'beingness'. For those people born in the wrong body, technological advances in the field of sexual transformation mean that, finally, some trans people may be brought into ontological and psychological existence, but this is not always an option. Julia Serrano (2013: 19) explains:

> While the medical establishment and the mainstream media typically define 'transsexual' in terms of the medical procedures that an individual might undergo (for example, hormones and surgeries), many trans people find such definitions to be objectifying (as they place undue focus on body parts rather than the person as a whole) and classist (as not all trans people can afford to physically transition).

Two major writers on the topic of transgender theory that are also important for us to consider are Leslie Feinberg and Kate Bornstein. Although I reference several works by both authors, the key texts I will draw upon in this study are Feinberg's *Transgender Warriors* (1996) and Bornstein's *Gender Outlaw: On Men, Women and the Rest of Us* (1994). *Transgender Warriors* is a virtual who's who of transgender history as the book outlines significant transgendered figures and lists them chronologically. The book also offers discussions on different experiences of gender and includes both transgender arguments: that of gender swapping and changing as a continual process and that of the essentialist view. Bornstein's *Gender Outlaw*, on the other hand, doesn't give such a stereoscopic view on transgender history, but rather focuses her discussion on her own personal experience of gender and performance. A gender performance artist and theorist, Bornstein conveys an analytical viewpoint on the transgender experience and is able to articulate her findings in a very informed and personable text. Feinberg and Bornstein are two very influential figures in transgender studies and both are able to identify not only what it means to be 'trans' but also the possibilities that 'trans', as a study or practice, can introduce to gender studies and performance.

4

Case Study – All-Female Julius Caesar

Phyllida Lloyd CBE is a British stage and film director who has directed several Shakespeare productions for both the RSC and SGT. Known predominately for her work directing films such as *Mama Mia!* and the *Iron Lady*, Lloyd has had a penchant for putting women centre stage throughout her career. In 2003 she directed an all-female *The Taming of the Shrew* at SGT starring Janet McTeer and Kathryn Hunter. The production received positive reviews despite the amount of criticism other all-female and selectively cast female-in-male-roles productions had endured.

Unlike other female directors that make work featuring women but deny that the work is 'feminist', Lloyd is comfortable with her pro-women status. She even called her biopic *Iron Lady* politically feminist and explained that it had a feminist agenda – 'this is a story about a woman struggling to make her voice heard in an all-male world' – and because it 'puts an old lady at the centre of the story' (Williams *The Metro* 2012). She even compares the storyline with that of Shakespeare's play about aging, displacement and waning power:

> It's a sort of King Lear story about a mighty leader who rises to power, against all the odds, who holds the line when others are losing their faith, who becomes a global superstar, and then – either through their own hubris, or, as they see it, the treachery of everyone around them – crashes to an ignominious end. (Cochrane *The Guardian* 2012)

Despite being doubly disadvantaged in the industry because of her own age and gender, Lloyd has paved the way for female-driven

33

projects to get the green light. Her film version of the musical *Mamma Mia!* not only provided many positive roles for women but also 'became the highest-grossing film of all time at the UK box office, proving beyond doubt that there was an enormous audience for female-led films, including those featuring women in their 50s and above' (Cochrane 2012).

Lloyd continues to have her finger on the pulse of the industry and isn't afraid to voice her political feminist views on the status of women and the lack of roles offered. In December 2012, she publically 'insisted that a paucity of roles for women in Shakespeare's plays was no excuse for not recruiting the same number from both sexes' (*The Telegraph* 2012). As reported by Rojas in *The Telegraph*, Lloyd also directly named and shamed the RSC stating that:

> I do think it's absolutely iniquitous that the RSC for example puts together a company at the beginning of a year that has so few women in it on the basis that, well, there are only these roles in Shakespeare plays, when actually what they should be doing, and probably the European Union will legislate soon … I would imagine, somebody's going to be shaming the theatre. They should be just told that they have to have a 50/50 employment spread, then work out how to do the plays. If that means some gender-blind casting, some all-female, some all-male, it's not rocket science, and I think they could have some fun. (2012)

This remark received press attention that served to place the issue at the forefront of industry discussions. However, some of these discussions were not necessarily woman-positive. Professor Michael Dobson of the Shakespeare Institute addressed Lloyd's statement in Peacock's *The Telegraph* (2012) article disagreeing that the RSC or any company should be forced to cast an equal number of male and female performers:

> There has to be some artistic exceptions to terms of employment law. We've got to allow directors to do what they think is right. Not all productions are going to be in an aesthetic range that will welcome cross-gender casting. Casting more women to play men could make it incoherent to a mainstream audience. (2012)

The RSC's Artistic Director Gregory Doran took the comment in his stride and recounted that the RSC has a history with cross-gender casting, commenting that the practice 'is something we've been doing in Stratford for years and these initiatives are now being taken up and expanded by others' (Rojas 2012). He also pointed out that the RSC 'plans to further explore the issues surrounding women in theatre, and a company with a 50:50 split of male and female actors is one that I've already challenged Phyllida to come and run in Stratford-upon-Avon' (Rojas 2012).

The issue is compounded by the fact that Shakespeare's plays do not allow for a diverse range or number of roles for women. *The Guardian* (2012) website has provided a detailed study on 'Shakespeare's Invisible Women' that is informative and interactive. The 'interactive guide maps out the facts by total numbers of roles, total numbers of lines and comparative percentages' breaking down the disparity logically to render the situation very clear. Elizabeth Freestone, one of the creators of the interactive guide, points out that 'Shakespeare of course wrote for all-male companies but his legacy has lived on and an analysis of his plays show that only 16% of the 981 characters he wrote were female' (*The Shakespeare Standard* 2012). Phyllida Lloyd's statements are bold but they certainly strike at the very heart of the casting controversy experienced not only in the UK but the USA as well.

In her controversial interview on the BBC with Will Gompertz (2012), Lloyd explained her decision to employ an all-female cast to bring *Julius Caesar* to the Donmar Warehouse stage in London. She explained that 'for every one job given to a girl in the London theatre three jobs go to boys' and she decided 'the time had come to make some reparation' (Gompertz 2012). But the project didn't begin with an all-female cast in mind. In 2012 two women took key positions at the Donmar Warehouse. Josie Rourke became the artistic director and Kate Pakenham was hired as the newly appointed executive director. The two directors approached Lloyd to direct a project for the theatre and, at first, she aimed to create a project that, with equal roles for all, 'makes the women in the audience feel included'. She later decided 'To hell with that! You've got to go much further' (*New York Observer* 2013) and her all-female concept was born in an effort not only to create more roles and role models for women in classical theatre but also to create theatre for all.

In the controversial BBC interview with Will Gompertz (2012), she discussed her decision to stage *Julius Caesar* with an all-female cast. Lloyd explained that the play contained several large and complex roles for actors to tackle and that working on it would be an adventure, stepping 'beyond the issue of all-female' casting, as its themes deal directly with 'eternal resonance' and potency. She also chose the play in order to cast women in leading powerful roles, explaining that, 'there's all kinds of territory in it which women rarely get to explore. Women are seldom wielding the knife or the axe' instead, in most classical productions women play characters that 'are somewhere back home putting the kettle on'.

At the start of the process the female actors in her production agreed with this point and expressed that, in terms of roles, they 'operate usually in a very narrow spectrum of what they are capable of'.[1] Female performers in the classical theatre predominately 'feel they have quite a small piece of the cake in a play and the rehearsal room'. In Lloyd's production the women were able to 'take up more space' which allowed them greater power and a richer overall rehearsal and performance experience; 'they get to cry out "Liberty, Freedom and Enfranchisement!"' discovering artistic territory formerly foreclosed to women. As Lloyd pointed out 'It's a new country for them' (Murray 2012).

Another reason Lloyd chose to stage *Julius Caesar* was because the play is a predominately male play and she wanted to turn its representation of gender on its head. Almost 50 of the characters in the play are male and two female, so rarely do women get the opportunity to perform in Shakespeare's highly charged political play. These roles also offer actors the opportunity to explore aspects of the human condition routinely denied to female performers such as violence, war, power and intrigue. Rarely do women get to take on roles as statesmen, military heroes and inspiring or notorious political figures as this is predominately seen as the territory of men. Tackling highly male narratives and such powerful roles, as offered in *Julius Caesar*, allows women to walk in different shoes, carving a new path for audiences.

This act of escaping gender shackles allows newly imagined possibilities not only of female actors in theatrical representation, but of all women's seemingly untapped political and social potential. If women can take such roles and play them well onstage, then it sets a precedence for them to do so offstage as well.

Lloyd has a vested interest in presenting women and leadership stories to the forefront. This was one of the reasons that she tackled the Margaret Thatcher biopic despite her own reservations and external opposition about doing so. Many people, particularly in the arts, were not fans of Thatcher; even Lloyd states that she had her reservations directing the piece. Nonetheless, she had 'been interested for a long time in exploring women and leadership'[2] (Price 2012: 21). However, the motivational factor to stage *Julius Caesar* with an all-female cast was a far easier decision:

> The point about this play is that they get to play everything, not just the love interest. They get to fill every single job in a world of politics and, as we say, Realpolitik – the world of pragmatic political operation. (Price 2012: 21)

For Lloyd, after presenting the *Iron Lady*, *Julius Caesar* was 'the next project on the desk' that would explore her passion to present women in leadership stories and she 'looked at a large number of Shakespeare plays before' (2012: 21) deciding to stage *Julius Caesar*.

Fairly early in the creative process Lloyd landed on the idea that the play might be set in a woman's prison. She interpreted the script in a way that led her to find that the main conspirators throughout the play 'feel that they are somehow prisoners of Julius Caesar and his Rome' (Murray 2012).

In order to test her concept of setting the play in a prison Lloyd and Actor Harriet Walter, playing the role of Brutus, led workshops on the play before formal rehearsals began with real female inmates at Holloway prison in London's Islington borough. The dramatic reality of these women's lives and experience was not lost on Walters but it also allowed her to reposition her thinking about her role:

> There are women in Holloway who have killed or have seen people killed – it's not like a softie bourgeoisie actor like me who hasn't been in that environment. But I can imagine myself into it more easily through the prison metaphor than jumping straight into ancient Rome. We visited prisons and talked to prisoners and the common humanity is what jumps out. (Price 2012: 27)

As Lloyd and Walters worked on the play with the women in the prison they asked the participants 'how' they were approaching the cross-gender roles. They wanted to discern if the women were playing the roles as men, as women or as women playing male characters. Intriguingly the women replied 'more the characters' (Murray 2012). This idea influenced Lloyd's approach to the theatrical portrayal of the genders in her production:

> In the scenes in which the issue of gender is clear – for example, where one of the characters has a wife – it's become very clear that

the person who is a husband is a man and the wife is a woman. But in other scenes we haven't focused on 'am I acting a man or a woman?' but more 'what's my character actually doing here?' (Price 2012: 22)

Walters admitted that in a heightened language play, like those of Shakespeare, she doesn't focus heavily on the gender of the character but takes her cues from the text. In her process for embodying Brutus she 'didn't think about the male thing too much' (Price 2012: 24). She began by constructing an image of her Brutus that allowed her to become more masculine 'like Antony Sher draws pictures of himself, I reached towards the image that I created, so I did have a vision of Brutus' (Price 2012: 24).

The rehearsal process

The rehearsal process facilitated by Lloyd was uniquely feminist and from all accounts harkens back to collaborative practice wherein the female participants not only participated in consciousness raising but each had an equal stake in the production, contributing skills and experience on an equal playing field. Many of the cast members discussed how usually in male-led and male-dominated rehearsals the process is far less empowering and they are generally given a 'smaller piece of the cake'. Jenny Jules expressed this sense of being secondary to men in the production process in an interview with Charlotte Higgins for *The Guardian* stating that women 'always have to be the side-monkey' and then went on to add 'OK, not always. But I find myself playing a lot of wives and girlfriends, or parts that support the men's meat-and-potato roles' (Higgins 2012).

Many of the actors described the rehearsal process as both a consciousness-raising experience and, equally importantly, an interactive one. They do not describe the experience as a process 'dictated' by Lloyd, but more as an open forum of collective debate predicated upon a sharing of questions, thoughts and experiences. This is indicative of feminist approaches to work and references past feminist consciousness-raising (CR) practice.

Feminist practice

Having a safe space for women to analyse and critique patriarchal and cultural politics was integral to feminist theatre practices that began in the 1970s. Inspired by women's CR groups, substantial all-women or women-focused companies began to form and create spaces 'of their own in which to share experiences, feelings, and problems that could not be expressed or were not considered important enough to be voiced in a mixed social or cultural context' (Aston 1999: 33). The female single-sex theatre environment became an essential response to the male-dominated spaces that made up the majority of theatre and theatre history. 'It was important to signal our focus on women. Men don't have to flag up men's theatre because theatre is that anyway' (1999: 23). Even theatre companies that started as mixed but with predominately women members, such as *Monsterous Regiment*, slowly became all-women:

> We realised that we had never worked in an all-women, as opposed to women-dominated, environment and we wanted to explore that. We found that it gave us a different kind of freedom to anything we had experienced before and we enjoyed it. (Hanna 1991: 1xii)

These women's theatre companies and feminist theatre projects, such as the *Women's Theatre Group, Foursight Theatre*, the *Women's Theatre Project*, and the *It's All Right to be Woman Theatre* integrated CR experiences with theatrical practices in much the same way that Lloyd and her cast explored *Julius Caesar*.

Although the *Julius Caesar* project wasn't focused upon creating women-centred material, it did raise the participants' awareness of social gender politics at play in our culture and on the women creating a theatrical response. Like the feminist CR groups of the past, the women-only context offered 'the opportunity for confidence building (in the absence of men)... and for prioritizing (their) creativity and experience as women' (Aston 1999: 25) which proved vital to their ability to feel safe to play the male roles. The women-only context also created an environment in which the women were no longer constrained by the oppressive patriarchal 'ideology that causes women to think of themselves as "objects" rather than "subjects", as passive rather than active, and as an effect of meaning rather than a producer of meaning' (Donkin and Clement 1993: 21).

The *Julius Caesar* participants repeatedly described the rehearsal and research process as empowering and liberating. Although the women involved in the project were from diverse backgrounds, spanning from the very seasoned Shakespearean actors to women with little to no classical training, the rehearsal room was 'wholly supportive' and everyone contributed their talents and expertise to the collective group. In her 'Rehearsal Diary' Hannah Price writes at the end of her week one description, 'The room feels like a safe place, non-judgmental, equitable and free' (Price 2012: 15). She later reiterates this sentiment across subsequent weeks:

> The room is open, honest and supportive. Anyone can chuck in an idea, suggest an amendment, ask for a new exploration to take place ... Personal experience is important too. Individuals bring ideas, experiences and stories. Phyllida is open to suggestion, harvesting the imaginative power of the group. (2012: 16–17)

Harriet Walter also discusses Phyllida Lloyd's feminist approach to directing in the rehearsal room expressing Lloyd's extraordinary ability to support her actors as they make dynamic theatrical choices. From her account, Lloyd leads through detailed observance of her actors and with quiet confidence:

> She takes responsibility and she's calm as well, so you don't feel any emotional obligation to support her in that way that you sometimes do in a rehearsal room – to support the director's ego. (2012: 26)

Instead of working from a place of hierarchal power, Lloyd's rehearsal room allows flexibility, freedom and experimentation. She 'has great courage' is 'inspirational' and approaches the rehearsal as 'an experiment that might not work' (2012: 26) which generates bold, fresh ideas to flourish. In her interview with Grace Henderson for *Aesthetica* (2012) Frances Barber also pointed out the diversity amongst the cast and the sense of experimentation in the rehearsal room:

> It's a very mixed multiracial cast of all ages and experience. I find this particularly thrilling as it's an opportunity to work with a fantastically talented group of women who are all encouraged to contribute on every level in the rehearsal process. We feel safe and protected enough to experiment without fear of failure as this is, after all, an experiment for us all.

In addition to the director and cast working to share their experience and talents, additional artists were brought into the rehearsal process to support the practical and creative aspects of the production. In order to help the women to understand how to perform outside their social gender prescriptive behaviour Ann Yee, a movement specialist, was enlisted to assist the women in improving their 'masculine' physicality. She began by training 'the cast to start accessing their energy with strength' and with exercises addressing 'fear and power, helping us to understand how they act on the body' (Price 2012: 15). In Eleanor Turney's feature (2013) actor Cush Jumbo describes the experience as playful and liberating, explaining that the women were taught to gruff up, take up space and be more physically dominant:

> It was really interesting to be in a room where we could all experiment and nobody was self-conscious about looking sweaty, looking ugly, speaking too loud, taking up too much space or any of that stuff. It was so freeing to run around, in a tracksuit, kicking the crap out of each other. It felt like being in the playground again.

In order to approach the 'prison violence' and the murder of Caesar in a strong and believable staging, fight director Kate Waters worked tirelessly with the cast on creating an environment wherein the violence was believable and even 'shocking' in the women's hands:

> On stage women are usually the victims of violence, not the perpetrators. The cast have to access their strength in new ways, create solid foundations from which to inflict pain. The impact of seeing this cannot be underestimated: shocking, raw physicality of an extreme variety. (Price 2012: 17)

Criticism of all-female productions in the past usually includes scathing remarks of how the female cast members approach a battle or combat scene in the play. In 2003 critical response to the all-female casting of *Richard III* and *Much Ado About Nothing* at SGT wasn't positive. Critic Benedict Nightingale compared the *Richard III* battle scenes to 'a hockey field brawl' and Charles Spencer poked fun at *Much Ado About Nothing* in the *Daily Telegraph* stating that 'a hen-night fight with handbags would be more exciting' (Klett 2009: 163). Lloyd's *Julius Caesar* production was reviewed far more favourably in both the London and NYC stagings.

Kate Bassett in *The Independent* (9 December 2012) wrote admirably about the company's approach to their masculinity and the play's violent edge, 'Barber and co indulge in their merciless violence, and Walters' craggy Brutus is an unsettlingly androgynous depressive' and Zachary Stewart in *Theatre Mania* (10 October 2013) declared that the violence was 'thrillingly conventionalized … until it becomes frighteningly real violence … we are never allowed to forget that these are inmates performing the play, with their own drama boiling just under the surface'.

Julius Caesar conclusion

Although we have yet to evaluate and uncover the long-term effects of this work on the industry, it is obvious that the immediate effects are already in motion and making a profound impact on women's visibility in Shakespeare. The women directly involved in the production view their participation in the industry quite differently than when they started the project. They wish to see themselves cast in greater roles including leading male roles and hope to challenge casting bias at the onset. They aim 'to just be given the chance to *chomp*' (Higgins 2012) on these major roles and find the unique casting to be richly rewarding. 'Having now had a taste of a male Shakespeare character I'd quite like to have a go at Macbeth as I love the poetry so much' (Henderson 2012). Cush Jumbo has designs on playing Hamlet in the future: 'he's a moany motherfucker, but that's because a man has always done it' (Higgins 2012). She also describes the cross-casting experience as one that has far more conscious effect than simply wanting to be cast in male roles, explaining that she would 'like to come to whatever role I do next without going back to my old, apologetic place' (2012).

It is also worth noting that the production gained serious press attention. The director and actors were interviewed and featured in countless news stories and across media formats. Women's status in the arts became a popular topic in 2012 and as a result of such exposure the production was a smashing success at the Donmar Warehouse in London. Tickets for the production sold out rapidly and I had to settle for on-the-day standing-room-only ticket – which was well worth the hours on my feet.

The success of the production in London led to it being the first New York transfer of a production from the Donmar under the management of Josie Rourke. Despite the fact that many all-male companies have been remounted in New York from London, including the Globe's recent *Twelfth Night* and *Richard III*, this was a first for an all-female Shakespeare production from London. The production was transplanted with nearly the entire cast to NY's St Anne's Warehouse and received more positive reviews and attention in the US:

> the critical reception to Caesar has proved less polarising than at the Donmar, with the production receiving the best reviews for any revival during the current New York season. (*London Evening Standard* 16 October 2013)

At the Donmar, the production ran for ten weeks and sold out a 250-seat house. In New York, the production sold out all tickets in its 2,500-seat theatre and even had to extend the US run. At its opening night the cast received a standing ovation and in the audience were powerhouse figures from the women's movement including playwright Eve Ensler of the Vagina Monologues and actor-activist Jane Fonda.

Michael Giltz of *The Huffington Post* (10 October 2013) proclaimed that it was 'the best *Julius Caesar* I've ever seen' and 'one of the top shows of the year', and Ben Brantley of the *New York Times* (9 October 2013) raved that 'For as biologically inapt as it may sound, this interpretation of one of Shakespeare's most manly tragedies, directed by Phyllida Lloyd, generates a higher testosterone level than any I have seen'. This praise was bestowed upon the production, despite the fact that New York critics are well accustomed to reviewing work by the many professional all-female and female-driven Shakespeare companies operating in New York City.

Lloyd's feminist approach to casting, and to the rehearsal process, yielded a plethora of fresh ideas and experiences that most female actors rarely are privy to in traditionally gendered Shakespeare. The prison concept allowed the women to set their imaginations in a tangible and sometimes violent world and at the same time afforded them liberties to play their parts in the play within the play and to experiment with gender in new explorations. It also gave the audience and critics a conceptual frame in which to paint such possibilities. The result is that we believe the fictions and representations as these blurring relationships, hierarchies, sexualities, genders and relations contain an edgy sense of realism inside the prison construction. As we are imprisoned in the theatre amongst the 'prisoners', surrounded by Bunny's authoritarian and encompassing set design, we become part of the play and enact our 'imaginary forces' and dare to believe these women are entrapped in *Julius Caesar's* political web. The cast's gender becomes mostly irrelevant as we each construct or deconstruct the presentation of gender in our minds.

Is this not the effect and reparation that Phyllida Lloyd aimed to stage? Without question the metaphorical imprisonment of women in an authoritarian system is ripened through this production. Perhaps there is something to be said further about the fact that it is only when the women take up the hallmarks of masculinity or play male roles that they are given status and power. Are we more likely to accept acts of violence and positions of power from women only if they assume the roles of men and that assumption is predicated on a sense of fiction? On a presumption that these women, at the end of the production, will go back to their usual place and put the kettle on?

Another idea to be explored in relation to the theatrical imprisoned metaphor and feminist analysis is that of the political structures that are represented and critiqued through the production and its processes. Creating a women-only space and project is a brave step and certainly merits our admiration but it also creates another type of political system that values the work of one group over another. Is there a danger inherent in this approach to incidentally become the very system you are fighting against? Perhaps that is the thematic lesson of Shakespeare's *Julius Caesar* and by extension Lloyd's production.

Lloyd's practice and approach to directing *Julius Caesar* can be seen as Intersectional in the way she integrates women from diverse cultures with differences in race, sexuality, status, class and age, but her exclusion of men in the process marks her work as not fully intersectional. Other directors featured in the volume such as Joanne Zipay and Lisa Wolpe fall into this category more easily. However, the processes by which Lloyd facilitated rehearsals as described by many of the actors denote strong feminist aesthetics – equality amongst all, the abolition of hierarchical structures, wherein actors, particularly women, rarely if ever get to make suggestions or experiment with their own ideas. Lloyd still commanded the rehearsal room but did so because of her experience and through winning the respect of her actors. Her collaborative approach meant that the actors took ownership of the production and this resulted in a richer investment in the project.

In her interview on BBC's 'Woman's Hour', Lloyd explains that the concept of using 'one gender or another whether it's all male or all female does help to somehow throw what the play is about in to really bold colours' (Murray 2012). However, all-female casting has an even greater strength for the industry as it allows women and minorities greater opportunities to work in the classical theatre. Intersectional approaches are predominately expressed in all-female productions as they seek to not just give women more opportunities, but do so regardless of race, class, age, ethnicity and disability. Casting beyond gender is also a blind and imaginative eye to lead other areas of the casting process, making more creative leaps imaginatively possible and with a richer outcome for all.

5
Opportunity in Performing Shakespeare is a Drag for Women

In terms of feminist theory and thinking, one of the key areas of consideration is the employability of women and equal access to jobs and pay. Of particular interest to many feminists is the notion that women should be treated equally in the industry, and assuming that she has the same qualifications and experience, a woman should receive the same opportunities and pay as her male colleague in the workplace. Of course, employment laws in countless industries require such equal treatment and have strict hiring practices and protocols as a result of previous equality battles long fought by feminists and 'fair pay and equal treatment' laws. However, the arts seem to be an area in which such laws are routinely disregarded.

It's difficult to imagine that discriminatory practices towards women would be accepted in our industry in this day and age, but unfortunately that is what appears to be happening. Arguments are being made as to how and why such disparity between men and women's access to employment in the arts exists as many don't see their practices as discriminatory and require guidance as to how to rectify the inequality. Despite a lack of clarity, the facts and figures speak volumes and studies in the field continue to shed light on this dim subject.

Two important studies have launched renewed focus on gender equality in the theatre and place a spotlight on the lack of opportunities presented for women in the classical theatre. These two studies were made in Europe and North America with varying responses to their accuracy and legitimacy. However, these studies seem to affirm what women already suspected and experienced – less opportunity, less visibility and little to no change in gender equality. In fact, this was discussed at BBASS[1] when actors male and female felt that we, as a culture, had 'stepped backwards' since the 1980s. Like women, other artists of diversity are routinely left behind in the industry. Shannon Gilreath in his book *Sexual Politics* (2006) describes the concept of attentive politics explaining that the project of equality is an ongoing political concern. Studies such as these regarding gender and other diversities are important as they help us to recognise where our aims for equality may be failing.

In the UK one of the biggest arguments for women's visibility in the classical theatre has come recently as a result of the European study launched in 2008 by Debra Dean at the University of Warwick. The aims of the study were 'to consider the effects of gender stereotypes and portrayal of women on employment opportunities for performers and on images of women in society in general' (Dean 2008: 5). This study also explored pertinent questions regarding equality of access to employment between men and women, as well as 'content of jobs, pay and career longevity' (2008: 5). The study polled over 2,000 performers across 21 European countries. The results were illuminating, but many felt that the findings were not surprising. Women were in the lowest income bracket and 'saw their gender as disadvantageous to them along every dimension (number and variety of roles, pay, ageing, 'type' most often cast as)' (2008: 5). Whereas men saw their gender primarily as an advantage and, as the study revealed, 'have longer careers as performers than women' (2008: 4).

This is perhaps one of the issues that Phyllida Lloyd is addressing in her urging of theatres throughout Europe to cast equally between men and women. Certainly we should be reconsidering the way we cast actors in traditional performances of Shakespeare. Shakespeare wrote his plays with an all-male cast in mind and actors he knew well in his company. There are arguments that, when writing his plays, the number of women's roles presented were based entirely on the number of boy players that his company had access to at that time. In the same way that he conceivably wrote comic clown characters for the comic actors in his ensemble, so too he wrote female parts for his boy actors. This practice worked well for Shakespeare and actors of his time, but to follow this practice today, in all-male or even gender and ethnic 'appropriate' castings, leaves an unequal share of opportunities for women and minority artists.

For many in the industry the answer seems simple and commissions more work from female writers to create more roles for women. However, it is estimated that in the United States only 17% of new plays produced are from women playwrights.[2] In *Opening the Curtain on Playwright Gender: An Integrated Economic Analysis of Discrimination in American Theatre* (2009) Emily Glassberg Sands at Princeton University reveals that there is 'ample evidence of all three forms of taste-based gender discrimination in theatre' (2009: 104) and that 'The severity of the discrimination against female playwrights appears to be more pronounced for women writing about women than for women writing about men' (2009: 104–5). And the equality issues do not stop there; speaking at the Judith Shakespeare Company panel discussion Maxine Kern stated grimly that the 'statistics on women directors right now is that of all the directing work (being) done' fewer than 20% of the productions staged are 'being directed by women. That statistic has been unchanged for the last twenty years' (Stokes 2005).

Statistics from the UK on the presence of women in key theatre positions such as acting, directing and writing are not much better. The Sphinx Theatre Company posts figures on their website (2014) that claim in the industry women make up 35% of all professional actors, 17% writers and 23% directors, despite the fact that women make up 52% of the population. Furthermore, women find their career opportunities as performers are doubly disadvantaged as they age and triply disadvantaged if they are of an ethnic minority:

> Principally, minority ethnic women performers perceive a triple burden (ethnicity, gender, ageing) in relation to employment issues ... they experience both multiple and intersectional disadvantage (perceptions of ethnicity compounded by 'aged' perceptions of gender). (Dean 2008: 5)

It is important to note that both studies indicate a general bias towards women's presence and roles that equate to less jobs and opportunities for female performance artists. Additionally these studies take in a larger genre of work including contemporary plays rather than looking exclusively at classical roles and Shakespeare. I suspect that if we were to look empirically at women's participation and employment in Shakespeare productions and roles such figures would be doubly appalling. Many female performers in the classical theatre continually report that there is a serious lack of roles and opportunities for women as many directors continue to cast using 'gender appropriate' processes.

Joanne Zipay, artistic director of the Judith Shakespeare Company in New York City, originally created her company to rectify this issue.

Zipay who 'once considered opportunities for women in classical theatre an oxymoron' (Wolper 1996: 24) uses cross-dressing and cross-gender casting 'to be more creative with the casting of women in classical theatre' (Zipay 2005: 16) and 'stake a claim for women within an existing tradition' (Wolper 1996: 24). At our meeting in 2005, Zipay shared her view that casting women in male roles creates professional opportunities for classically trained female actors normally rejected by producers and directors. 'In the average Shakespeare play there are only two female roles to every ten male ones. Yet there are hundreds of classically trained female actors auditioning and struggling to get those parts. If we continue to cast based on sex, women will never work.'[3] And she is not alone in this sentiment. Director Erin Merritt formerly of the all-female Woman's Will in San Francisco recounted that before starting her company she would audition for female Shakespeare roles competing with countless numbers of women. 'We'd have 50–100 women up for one role' and that the casting was based on which male actors were chosen and which female actor 'looks good with them' (Brinklow 2012).

Casting women in male roles seems to be a good step forward in making more opportunities for women to be evermore present and visible in productions of Shakespeare, but gender biases appear to infiltrate in this approach as well. At the Actor's Equity Association's panel discussion 'Limitless Casting: Could the Best Man for the Part Be a Woman?', Gail Schaeffer pointed out that even cross-gender casting contains a double standard as many publications 'celebrate men doing roles in drag, or female cast male, but not the other way around' (Nestor 2011). Director and actor Lisa Wolpe has been working with all-female Shakespeare casts and playing many of Shakespeare's leading male roles for over 20 years. When seeking funding for the Los Angeles Women's Shakespeare Company's *Hamlet* in 2013, she received comments from potential sponsors such as 'That sounds like a gimmick' (Derr 2013).

And the double standard doesn't stop there. Women working with Shakespeare and gender, such as Wolpe and Zipay, are not fully respected as their work is deemed less 'legitimate' or as accomplished as their male peers. Wolpe describes this under-evaluation of her expertise and talent:

> People always talk to me like, 'So, could this be applicable in the third grade? Maybe we could strengthen the girls in the Christmas pageant.' Stop infantilizing me because I'm female. Ian McKellan and I have sat and talked about our Richard III. I know as much as anyone. It's not different. We are doing exactly the same thing as Kevin

Spacey, who runs a theater company and played Richard III, but nobody asks Spacey if he's thought about doing it with high-school students. It's just that you expect me to be different, like someone who doesn't want all that. (Derr 2013)

Many female performers face similar frustrations as Wolpe and have fought against the 'male-dominated' establishment for roles, respect, equality and legitimacy for decades. The practice of casting women in male roles is routinely regarded in the UK and USA as an 'experiment',[4] 'taboo' (Goodman 1998: xxiii), 'meaningless'[5], and is usually met with far sharper scepticism and critique than the practice of casting men in female roles. Reviewer Charles Spencer of *The Telegraph* (5 December 2012) quibbles that before he attended Phyllida Lloyd's all-female *Julius Caesar*:

> I vowed that I wouldn't resort to Dr Johnson's notorious line in which he compared a woman's preaching to a 'dog's walking on his hind legs. It is not done well, but you are surprised to find it done at all'.

Consider that the same reviewer in *The Telegraph* (19 November 2012) bestows the highest of praise for SGT all-male productions of *Richard III* and *Twelfth Night*, practically declaring Mark Rylance a Shakespearean deity:

> Watching him at full stretch, as he is in this sensational double-bill of productions first seen over the summer at Shakespeare's Globe, I found myself recalling the poet Gerard Manley Hopkins's rapt description of a falcon in flight: 'the achieve of, the mastery of the thing'.

Mark Rylance is, in my opinion, an exceptional actor and his portrayals of both *Richard III* and Olivia in *Twelfth Night* are stellar and deserving of praise, but so too are the mercurial performances of the *Julius Caesar* cast. Spencer is clearly far more accepting of the all-male productions, even emphasising the benefit of the cross-cast playing:

> It is wonderful to see this sad but also absurd figure waking to the wonder of love, entirely unaware that the youth he falls for is actually a woman in disguise, a deception given added piquancy in this 'original practices' production by the fact that, as in Richard III, all the female characters are played, superbly, by men. (2012)

Many critics seem to fall into this double standard, praising the single-sexed productions or cross-cast roles by men and unabashedly criticising the trope in reverse.

In the UK, criticism of women's cross-dressed performances in male roles has been so harsh it has been known to create deep-seated anxieties in female performers. Consider, for example, the sharp criticism the award-winning Fiona Shaw received when she took the male lead in *Richard II* directed by Deborah Warner at *The National Theatre* in 1995. This was a groundbreaking production of *Richard II*; nevertheless, Shaw's performance garnered the bulk of the attention from critics who deemed her king 'a disastrous performance in the main role' (*Sunday Telegraph* 14 June 1995), 'a Drag' (*The Daily Mail* 16 June 1995) and 'unconvincing as an anointed king of England' (*The Independent* 5 June 1995) and proclaimed that 'Shaw doesn't have enough maleness to play Peter Pan' (*The Independent*). Shaw describes the difficult experience in her foreword in Goodman's *The Routledge Reader in Gender and Performance* (1998), explaining that she had 'no idea then how great the taboo was that I was breaking' (Goodman 1998: xxiii) in playing a 'man' and masculinity on the English stage. Despite the fact that Shaw's performance has been cited as 'ground breaking' and has paved the way for women to play male roles on the English stage, in interviews on the experience she fervently expresses her decision to never play outside her gender again.

Audiences and funders have a tendency to fall into a critical pattern as well, making all-female or cross-gender castings of women in male roles financial risky business. As a result, such productions remain in smaller theatres, with less visibility and limited runs, and systemically unviable. Many of the all-female companies surveyed in this study are struggling to fund their work and to retain their audiences' interest. Many have reduced their schedules and require actors and production artists to volunteer their services, and a few have disbanded or are on the cusp of doing so. Additionally, these companies are overlooked and remain largely on the periphery of the industry.

Clearly there is evidence that there is a gender bias at work in our industry. So why is this happening? There are several arguments as to why such gender discrimination is prevalent but primarily it seems to be, as feminists have argued for decades, a socio-psychological effect of living in a patriarchal culture. In their *Report on the Status of Women: A Limited Engagement*, Jonas and Bennett attempt to analyse the alarming under-representation of women in theatre. Throughout their report they give many examples of possible reasons for the gender disparity, even referencing Dr Virginia Valian's socio-psychological work *Why So Slow?* (1999):

> According to Valian's research, both women and men share the same consistent subconscious over-valuation of the work of men and under-valuation of the work of women ... they are acting on deep assumptions that are neither equitable nor accurate.[6]

This analysis suggests that it is not only men that deem women's work of lesser importance and quality than men's, but that women are just as complicit in rendering women's work in theatre unequal. Indeed, one of the most controversial findings from the Glassberg Sands study in 2009 revealed that female artistic directors and managers judged female playwrights' submissions with harsher scrutiny than male submissions. Her findings revealed:

> Scripts bearing female pen-names are deemed by artistic directors to be of lower overall quality and to face poorer economic prospects than otherwise identical scripts bearing male pen-names. In addition, artistic directors believe cast and crew will be less eager to work on a female-written script. Female artistic directors, in particular, deem scripts bearing female pen-names to be poorer fits with their theaters, and to face not only worker discrimination, but also customer discrimination. (2009: 104)

Another possible reason for such harsh criticism of women in the field comes as a result of an unconscious fear of women holding positions of power or deeply held beliefs that only men can be authoritative figures. Such (author)itative roles would include those in the field of playwriting, directing, producing and acting. Women taking the stage in highly charged political and powerful male roles, even as a theatrical device, seems to unseat male patriarchal power beyond the stage and threaten prescriptive notions of male gender privilege. Professor James C. Bulman explains that it's unsettling for the audience because 'women typically aren't associated with that kind of power, that kind of dominance' and actor Cush Jumbo of Lloyd's *Julius Caesar* agrees, 'I guess it's a little bit scary to see girls running around with so much power' (Soloski 2013).

Another reason for such disparity between opportunities presented and perceptions of work between male and female performers may also be a result of long-standing gender-biased casting practice. Casting associates and artistic directors can still cast according to gender, age and ethnicity as dictated by Shakespeare's text, despite the fact that doing so mostly results in minority discrimination. There is little to no regulation on theatre companies to adhere to the same strict guidelines for equality in hiring processes as there are in other employment sectors. When criticism is given about such casting practices the rebuttal is usually couched in arguments around 'creative license'. Certainly there are companies combatting these issues; many are featured throughout this book, but we must be prudent and not allow 'creative license' to become a licence to discriminate.

British Equity is shedding light on this topic and has launched campaigns to put pressure on the industry to treat men and women equally in terms of employment and access to jobs. In 2011 the Equity Women's Committee conducted research on the status of women's employment in theatrical roles at prominent subsidised theatres during the 2009/10 season. Like many of the previous studies mentioned, the results were abysmal as women were once again overshadowed by men. Of the 36 theatres polled 30 reported hiring significantly more men than women and one of the worst offenders was Shakespeare's Globe, with a reported 57 men and 14 female performers hired that season.[7] As a result of the study British Equity has requested that Arts Council England 'introduce comprehensive and transparent monitoring of casting in subsidised theatre so that the imbalance of roles for women and men can be addressed'.[8]

In an interview on Radio Ulster's 'Arts Extra', Equity Vice President Jean Rogers and Council Member Maggie Cronin discussed the status of women in the industry. Rogers stated that in subsidised repertory theatre the balance is at best two actors for every one actress. 'Unfortunately, looking back over 40 years, it has not got better and I think it has got worse in the last 10 years' (Equity website, 2014).

References to a degeneration in equality of opportunity for women and other minority artists in theatre and the entertainment industry were routinely echoed in the interviews I conducted and amongst my research findings. In the roundtable discussion of artists at the BBAS symposium held at Warwick University in 2013, many of the actors discussed their experience of a decreasing equality focus for employment in the sector. Dr Martha Lauzen's study on the Celluloid Ceiling (2013) analysis of women's presence revealed that not only are women still no better off than they were 16 years ago but their status has become worse:

> The film industry is in a state of what might be called *gender inertia*. There is no evidence to suggest that women's employment in key

roles has improved over the last 16 years. I think Manohla Dargis got it right when she told *Variety* recently, 'Hollywood is failing women' and 'Until the industry starts making serious changes, nothing is going to change.' (Silverstein 2014)

In his article for *American Theatre*, Richard Schechner (2010) shares a similar concern for the theatre particularly in terms of roles for women in the Western canon:

There are more great roles in the theatre for men than for women. For every Ophelia and Gertrude there are Hamlet, Claudius, Polonius, Laertes, Rosencrantz and Guildenstern, Gravediggers, the Ghost; for every Mother Courage and Kattrin, there are a Chaplain, Cook, Swiss Cheese, Eilif, Sergeant, Colonel and General. In most other areas of political, professional and aesthetic life, women are claiming their place, but not as much in theatre.

His point is made evermore poignant as he points out that the Western canon repertory 'is hugely over-balanced in favor of men's roles' and will remain so 'because the repertory is just that: works that are produced again and again'. He goes on to argue that cross-gender and 'blind' casting is a way forward to create opportunities where none currently exist and details the history of the genre to make his case, but he admits:

It would be attacked by both orthodox theatregoers and critics who are attached to realism of one kind or another, and by those who insist that gender cannot simply be wished away.

As I pointed out earlier, this is precisely what many performers are experiencing as they play with gender in the works of Shakespeare. However, there are notable exceptions of true acceptance of the form, and differences are apparent in the way such projects are reviewed and received in North America and the UK. Clearly, the more we play with gender as a trope, the closer we get to a more equal social and theatrical model.

So how might we combat this imbalance in roles and opportunities between men and women?

One argument is for the creation of more roles for women through new writing initiatives. Many companies are fostering new works including the Judith Shakespeare Company and the Oregon Shakespeare Festival.

Artistic director Joanne Zipay launched *Resurgence*, a playwriting plat-form for new work written in heightened language that significantly features roles for women. In their one year of running the initiative her team received over 300 plays, and several were selected for a staged reading and possible further development. In addition to holding such initiatives, many playwrights, dramaturgs and companies have devel-oped adaptations, revisions and appropriations of Shakespeare's plays. For example, *Desdemona: A Play About a Handkerchief* written by Paula Vogel, Shakespeare and Company's *Women of Will: The Complete Journey* and David Greig's *Dunsinane* produced by the RSC that focuses on Lady Macbeth's quest for the throne following her husband Macbeth's demise. However, as Schechner (2010) points out, 'no matter how many worthy new plays are written, the classic Western repertory continues to be played' and Shakespeare is a primary player in the repertory.

Another possibility is to place greater demands on our entertain-ment unions and subsidised theatres to give fair and equal treatment in hiring and to be diligent in offering a more balanced casting pro-file. This would include transparent casting procedures and outcomes, with companies being held accountable for any imbalances. A positive approach should also include blind casting, wherein the most talented actor would be cast in each role available regardless of their 'difference'. Schechner points out the benefits of this approach to casting:

> First, it would give actors the chance to play roles that have been off limits by virtue not of skills but because of gender, race, age or body type. Second, it would drive a wedge between actor and character, encouraging spectators and performers to critically examine interact-ing performance texts rather than assuming a simple-minded identi-fication of the performer with the role. Third, it would further stress the already weakened link between theatre and realism. Fourth, per-formers and spectators alike would be more able to see gender, race, age and body type not as 'biological destinies' but as flexible, histori-cally conditioned performative circumstances. (2010)

It is important to note that blind casting does not always result in women and minorities getting the biggest roles. Joanne Zipay discussed how preconceptions in casting caught her by surprise during her blind casting for *Cymbeline*; sometimes the best actors for male roles are men, and for female roles are women. However, the opportunity to see beyond gender and our assumptions about 'roles' at the start of the casting process would greatly benefit the industry and allow for more creative discoveries to be made.

Another way to make more opportunities for women in Shakespeare could be to allow the use of advanced technologies and other mediums to do some creative magic with roles. Intermedial performance can help stretch the audience's imagination and leap fully into a future that repositions gender in news ways. For example, director Alison Humphries at the University of Toronto worked on *A Midsummer Night's Dream* that used motion capture technology to digitally create some of the characters in the play. These digital figures were projected onto screens behind the actors playing the roles and the results were fascinating. Suddenly it was obvious that the sex, age, ethnicity and natural shape of an actor wasn't important for the role but rather their physical, vocal and imaginative capabilities were essential. Serving as digital puppeteers, the actors orchestrated the theatrical experience through technological illusory performances. This leap from Shakespeare into digital mocap performance may seem a stretch, but for many professional actors working in the film industry it is just a matter of time before the theatre catches up. Andy Serkis has won many awards and accolades for his digital creature creations and continued work in the field of 'cyber-thespianism'. He, and many others working in this area of acting, are classically trained actors and the fusion seems to fit quite naturally.

Above all we need to be far more conscientious in our approach to presenting gender and acknowledge that we operate primarily from residual patriarchal bias – conscious or unconscious. Becoming more aware of this fact is a positive step forward. If we assume that Dr Virginia Valiant's theory is correct, that we undervalue the work of women and prioritise men's efforts, then we must all be held accountable and make reparations. We should request far more diligence from key stakeholders in terms of creating equal casting opportunities, our evaluation of performances, our archival focus, our funding of work and envisioning our theatrical future.

Personal activities and political actions can be developed by teachers, artists, companies, audiences and funding bodies. The more visible and present we make current work that rebalances the disparity for women and minorities, the more others will follow that lead and dare to dream a different future. Female actors choosing male monologues, companies using gender-blind casting techniques, regendering of characters, reimagings and adaptations, selective castings and gender-swapping productions are tools for such change.

These approaches are more than just a creative way to stage Shakespeare – more than just 'a gimmick'. They are the instruments of an ongoing historical cross-gender practice, as well as a positive means whereby we can stretch the audiences' imagination, refresh Shakespeare's canon and create equal opportunities for women and minority artists. I hope by the end of this book I will have convinced you of this fact and inspired you to follow these bold footsteps.

Part II
In Practice

6
All-Male Companies

'All the world's a stage, and all the men and women merely players. They have their exits and their entrances, and one man in his time plays many parts' (Jacques, *As You Like It* Act II, Scene iv). Early modern theatre in England was predominantly performed by all-male companies, and in these companies the actors played all the roles, male and female. Shakespeare was an actor, playwright and shareholder in several professional single-sex male companies including the Lord Chamberlain's Men, the Queen's Men, the King's Men and perhaps, several others (Thomson 1999). These companies were composed of only men and boy players, because women were 'banned' or rather 'dissuaded' from performing professionally on stage, because conservative Elizabethans 'found the practice opprobrious' and felt that actors and the art of acting 'breaks with religious orthodoxy and inappropriately inspires lust in the observer' (Lublin 2012: 67).

The acting profession was not respected as it is today, and life as an actor, from surviving accounts, seemed extraordinarily difficult. Most companies struggled to find patrons and had to endure long tours through the provinces when the static theatres in the cities were closed due to outbreaks of the plague. Touring meant lengthy absences from families and loved ones and harsh travel conditions across rough terrain in abominable English weather. As described in Schoone-Jongen's *Shakespeare's Companies,* touring was considered by the London companies as 'an uncomfortable, dirty, grueling and not especially rewarding activity undertaken only to offset London misfortunes' (2008: 43).

Intolerable conditions and moral proscription are possible explanations for the absence of women's presence on stage in Elizabethan London, but they are not the only arguments being offered presently. Although it has been previously thought that women were legally 'banned' from the stages during this time period and therefore 'boy players' were a necessary replacement, new scholarship has emerged to challenge this point.

Jessica Schiermeister tackles this theory in her article for the *Shakespeare Standard* (2015). She states that 'as of now, no coherent argument has emerged to explain why women were excluded from the early modern English commercial stage', and from her research on the topic, she found no laws 'that state women were legally barred from performing on stage' in England during the Elizabethan period. She gives several reasons for women's absence including the point that notions of gender and definitions of 'boys' were very different from today.

My sense is that it wasn't a profession that women would choose in mostly conservative early modern England. According to Andrew Gurr in *Playgoing in Shakespeare's London* (2004), women attended the theatre, but as the remonstrance demonstrates the theatre was not a socially appropriate place for women unless accompanied by genteel men and therefore would not be a popular career choice, but as Orgel (1996) points out, they did perform privately or on rare occasions. Most likely women did not appear on stages publically as a result of cultural taste. Elizabethan England enjoyed a male-dominated transvestite theatre, and the boy player was at the heart of this art form.

The boy players

In response to the absence of women, early modern theatrical practice included boy players, usually young men, hired to play many of the female roles written into the plays, dances and jigs of the period. Bulman explains in *Shakespeare Re-Dressed* that cross-dressing was 'rooted in practical necessity' (2008: 23) and although there was conservative criticism around the homo-social nature of the companies and feared links between the cross-dressing of boys and homosexual behaviour, the theatrical practice was largely accepted and popular. Indeed, cross-dressing young boys was not only a theatrical practice of the time but a social one as well, if we are to review the practice with contemporary notions of gender performance. In his paper 'Love's Labours Bewildered!' (2010) Ronan Patterson points out that our readings and perceptions of gender are very different from those of the Elizabethans and are therefore a problematic area of historic criticism. He explains that all young children were dressed alike in 'dresses' and that:

> Boys wore dresses for their first few years. Boys were then 'breeched', given their first set of masculine clothes, in a ceremony which over

the years grew into a significant rite of passage. Boys would be given gifts and money at this time, in the way that children nowadays receive money for a First Communion or a Bar Mitzvah. In their earliest years it was almost impossible to tell the boys from the girls.

In addition to a conflicting definition of gender and a misunderstanding of cross-dressing as a practice, the term 'boy' in 'Boy Player' is also problematic. Many contemporary readers may envision young boys or male youths in the roles of Juliet, Ophelia and Cleopatra, but scholars argue that the age a young man was defined as a 'boy', and even the term itself, has differing associations and meanings from today. Although scholar David Kathman as quoted in Stanley Wells' article for the *New Theatre Quarterly* 'finds no evidence that any young person over the age of eighteen ever played a female before the Restoration' (2009: 174), Wells reviews the number of female roles in Shakespeare's plays and the number of known boy players in his company at the time the plays were written to draw conclusions about other possible castings. Through this process he 'tests the assumption that women's parts were sometimes played by grown men' (2009: 174) taking into account that doubling roles was a usual practice for companies of the period.

Some scholars argue that older actors playing female roles are indicated specifically in Shakespeare's text. In *A Midsummer Night's Dream* (Act 1 Scene ii) Flute declares that he can't play a woman because 'I have a beard coming' and the witches, often referred to as the 'bearded women' in *Macbeth*, point to older actors playing these female roles. Other scholars such as Orgel and Wells argue that leading actors would have been reluctant to give up major female roles to younger players. Others, such as Patterson, reference studies that have found that Elizabethan boys' voices broke later than that of today's youth, citing difference in diet and hormonal changes over the centuries. This possibly meant that a boy player could perform roles for a longer career length, maybe even into his late teens and early twenties.

Although we cannot empirically prove or disprove these arguments, they have a kind of cache in terms of contemporary practice. For example, SGT is known for its use of 'original practices' and has made the casting choice to use young male actors playing female roles *alongside* older male actors doing so also, part of their theatrical practice. In so doing, they set the company on the side of the 'older' actor/boy player argument. However, there is an implication of 'authority' coming from SGT, and the impression on audiences is that this is historically accurate. Stanley Wells feels strongly that the case is not so. In his conclusion he asserts that his 'survey of the boys' roles in Shakespeare's plays supports the contention that women's roles were always played by boys, and that it also demonstrates Shakespeare's professional skill in cutting his coat according to his cloth' (2009: 177).

SGT and the all-male approach

SGT, sometimes called the New Globe, was envisioned as a recreation of SGT by American actor Sam Wanamaker and built on a parcel on land in Southwark London, not far from where the original Globe Theatre and The Rose once stood. The aims of SGT are educational as well as entertaining: to reconsider the historic conditions of Shakespeare's premiere playing space and, through scholarship and creative envisioning, foster a historic theatre experience that might lead to new understandings and encounters with Shakespeare's plays.

A primary aim for the company is experimenting with 'original practices' and creating 'historic conditions' both in terms of architectural design, environment, materials and, most pertinent to our discussion, approach to performing the works of Shakespeare before audiences. However, before the company could recreate the original practices of performance, they had to build the site and recreate the historical environment that encircled Shakespeare's early modern actors. They had to build a Globe Theatre once again.

> Shakespeare's Globe was opened in 1997 on the site of the original theatre, which was destroyed by fire in 1613. Although it champions new interpretation and writing, Shakespeare's Globe emphasises the notion of 'original practice', a principle that starts with the building itself: it was reconstructed using the most authentic methods possible.[1]

The SGT Globe playhouse was built based upon research from contemporary scholarship and the advice of historical advisors as they attempted to use materials and architectural designs similar to those of the original Elizabethan theatres. As few surviving records or design plans were found detailing the original Globe's structure the Shakespeare Globe Trust, headed by Sam Wanamaker and architect Theo Crosby, relied primarily upon documents and materials from a variety of period sources to draw their initial building plans. They found inspiration from sources such as the panorama etchings of 1600s London by John Norden and Wenceslaus Hollar, a detailed drawing of the Swan Theatre made by Johannes Dewitt from his account of visiting London in 1595 and discoveries made from excavations of the Rose Theatre, found only blocks away from the reconstructed Globe site.

The company continues to attend to such great historical detail in their use of setting, costume and make-up design to aid their productions as well. Equally, SGT attempts to recreate a historic theatrical practice for the acting and staging of the plays in the Globe's recreated space, but this endeavour proves problematic as little to no accounts or evidentiary guidelines on such ephemeral aspects of theatricality exist. The company has to rely on the guidance of specialist scholars to give their best 'educated guess', and therefore their work primarily is an experiment as these ideas are tested in situ with the space and its audiences (Carson and Karim-Cooper 2008).

Cross-dressing roles and the use of 'boy players' are practical research areas in their experimental approach to performance at SGT. As the actors inhabit these roles, particularly that of Shakespeare's female characters, the audience is given a glimpse of how cross-dressing in theatrical practice may have been performed on Shakespeare's stage 'originally'. Catherine Silverstone (2005) explains:

> Not only do its actors operate within a history of Shakespearean performance but, in the original practices productions, they can be read as embodying the characters/actors of the early modern stage, tantalizingly offering the audience and actors the illusion of attending Shakespeare's theatre. (2005: 20)

In 2002, under the artistic direction of Mark Rylance, SGT began to experiment with gender in performance as part of their historic practice. The key production that sparked this emphasis in their approach was *Twelfth Night* directed by Tim Carroll. The production featured an all-male cast and the mercurial Rylance in the role of the Countess Olivia, playing in tandem with a younger 'boyish' actor in the role of Viola. This juxtaposition of older seasoned male actors playing in female roles alongside younger male actors also playing female roles is what sparked the scholarly debate about whether or not mature actors performed female roles on Shakespeare's stage. Marvin Rosenberg in *Shakespeare Bulletin* wrote in 2001 that:

> When I first began to study Shakespeare's plays, with my own experience of the theatre in mind, I simply could not accept the image of a stripling, however precocious, sustaining Shakespeare's increasingly complex, weighty women's roles against experienced

male players in perhaps the greatest acting company the world has known. (2001: 5–6)

The *Twelfth Night* production in 2002 seemed to demonstrate this idea for many critics and the offering of an alternative view to Kathman and Wells' claims that all female roles were played by 'boys' seemed far more palatable and even plausible when staged by SGT. Additionally, the all-male/older-younger actor approach to *Twelfth Night* foregrounded the homoerotic undercurrent ripe in the text and the rich layers of gender performativity. A young boy player as the cross-dressed Viola woos 'an older man in the guise of an aging woman' (Rose 2008: 223) and this theatrical effect is not only comical as the audience is aware of the ironies in the gender playing presented, but equally subversive as it challenges gender and sexual norms through the mask of theatre.

> In contemporary productions, with women playing the female roles, the attraction between Olivia and Viola/Cesario is often elided, while Orsino's interest in Cesario becomes almost normalized; the audience 'knows' after all, that Cesario is really a woman. In contrast, the all-male Globe production in period costume brought the complexities of the depiction of gender in the play into sharp focus. Moreover, the single-sex cast in their 'authentic' costumes and makeup brought the nuances of *Twelfth Night's* homoerotic implication to light on a number of different levels, in one sense *performing* the theatrical intricacies of such attractions, unexpectedly providing a corporeal rationale for critical arguments about Shakespeare's manipulation of gender norms. (2008: 211–12)

The 2002 production was a brave and successful endeavour as it received 'nearly unanimous' (2008: 210) praise from critics in London and New York. Following on from this success, productions in the 2003 season focused on single-sex configurations of actors and two companies amongst the ensemble were formed: the Men's Company and the Women's Company. The Men's Company opened the season with an all-male *Edward II* by Christopher Marlowe, followed by *Richard II*. The Women's Company tackled the all-female *The Taming of the Shrew* and *Richard III*. The season became known as the Regime Change and for many critics, audiences and scholars, the productions not only presented a historical glimpse at original practice, but challenged notions of contemporary gender stereotypes by presenting women in the single-sex Elizabethan practice.

The Women's Company received harsher criticism than the Men's Company, a point I will discuss in the next chapter, but it is important to note that gender performativity as 'original', 'authentic' and 'experimental' became an area of focus and attention in the SGT productions whilst Mark Rylance was artistic director. Upon his departure from the position, there was a decreased emphasis on single-sex productions, and attention was placed on new writing, adaptations and translations, another area of focus for the company.

In 2012 SGT remounted *Twelfth Night* with an all-star cast that included Mark Rylance reprising the role as Olivia and cast additions such as Stephen Fry as Malvolio. The remounted production stirred a renewed emphasis on gender and single-sex productions at SGT and another all-female *The Taming of the Shrew* was produced. When approached about the emphasis on original practices and the selection of an all-male cast for *Twelfth Night*, director Tim Carroll explained to reporter Matt Trueman:

> I can see how lopsided classical plays are for men and women. There's no doubt that's a very regrettable thing, particularly galling for all the amazing actresses over 40. But I don't feel the need to justify original practices on those grounds, because [original practice] is a very strong, clearly defined task. (*The Independent* 2012)

The success of that task is evident in the performances as a result of SGT's company approaches the cross-dressing practice with a sincere rigour particularly evidenced in the performances of the actors playing female roles. In a 2012 article in *The Independent,* actor Johnny Flynn describes his approach to playing the roles of Viola in *Twelfth Night* and Lady Anne in *Richard III*:

> You've got to get that vocal range, expressive not sing-songy falsetto, your walk changes and you can't just sit in a chair, because you've got these skirts and a train.

Flynn has the experience of working in the all-male company Propeller to draw upon and even makes comparisons to the cross-gender preparatory training to that of an athlete but admits that the companies have very different aesthetic approaches to playing the female characters. Speaking about Propeller director Ed Hall's approach, Flynn shares that 'Ed doesn't ask his men playing women to put on a girly voice. They might be in a dress and some lipstick, but you still see bald spots and chest hair'.

The SGT approach to the cross-gender playing is far more immersive and nuanced. In an interview for Broadway World with Henderson (2013), actor Paul Chahidi described the demands of the SGT approach recanting hours of preparation, not just in the rehearsal room, but in the layers of make-up and costuming needed to transform him into Maria.

> I felt a huge responsibility ... There are precious few women's roles in classical theater, so if I was going to take this part, I wanted it to be real, not an over-the-top drag act.

In an online video posted on *Vimeo* by SGT in 2014 Paul is assisted by award-winning costume designer Jenni Tiramini and demonstrates the craftsmanship, detail, and process his 'layering' of costume and make-up create. He explains that as he gets into his layers of costume and extreme make-up (white foundation, red lips and accentuated eyebrows) he begins to sense a transformation into a sense of 'other'.

This crossing into a new gendered state is completed when his final dressing layers happens in front of the audience at the pre-show of the play in candlelight. 'A big part of the transformation', he explains, is the process of layering the technologies of costume and make-up. His shoes are heeled and at the beginning of the video, when he places them on his feet, he states that he is 'already feeling very different from the person who walked into the theatre an hour before in jeans and trainers'.

Costume designer Tiramini points out that the corset Chahidi wears under his many layers of dress is curved to give him 'a lovely womanly shape and hold his waist in as well'. The ruff he adorns around his neck is delicate, frames his face and gives his features a sense of femininity. He finds the act of placing the wig on to be 'the most important final element' to his transformation, giving him 'status along with the clothing' and full licence to play the female role.

It is interesting to note the meticulous process of preparation and transformation that these modern 'boy/man players' subject themselves to at SGT. As a comparison, their approach is similar to that of one of the oldest cross-gender performance forms still in practice – that of the Onnagata performers of the kabuki theatre in Japan. The Onnagata performers are 'male actors specializing in female roles' (Fujita and Shapiro 2006: 1) and first emerged on the stage in order to replace female artists when women were banned from performing publically in Japan in 1629 (2006: 1–5). The Onnagata's process of preparation is as rigorous as the SGT example, but the female roles are not played to the same effect. Kabuki Onnagata artists 'are not concerned with the imitation of a real woman' (2006: 181). Instead they work with gender and theatrical semiotics to hide the male body behind the stylised performance:

> In relation to costume, for example, there is a code by which every wig corresponds to a certain role. Meanings are decided, so that when a certain wig is worn, or certain make-up or kimono used, we know what kind of woman is being portrayed. (181)

This is not to say that SGT actors strive to imitate real women, but their approach and performances are constructed with a sense of 'natural' gender codes recognised by audiences, conveying a physical and psychological representation of Elizabethan women.

> Cross-dressing is of course an important element in what is going on, but 'Femininity' – and indeed 'Masculinity' – are constructed through voice, gesture and other performance codes which relate to (but may not be identical to) real-life gender stereotyping and real-life behavior. (2006: 23)

The emphasis for these actors is on the acting more so than on the costuming. The actors construct characters that convey a sense of life through their creative use of voice, movement and emotional depth. This is a clear distinction for the company from the performances of the Onnagata, and from other cross-gender company approaches such as that of Propeller, and one of the hallmarks of the company that makes their cross-gender performances some of the best on stage today. Writing about Rylance's performance of Olivia in *The New Yorker* (25 November 2013) it is clear that Hilton found the cross-gender playing extraordinarily presented:

> Rylance is an actor of remarkable gifts, alert to every moment, down to the wax dripping off the candles. When Olivia is away from Viola, his voice is all whispery disdain; when she's in the same room as her beloved, his vocal cords relax and his throat opens, rounding his sounds. And you can barely believe what he's able to express with his body. Small and trim, his skirts swinging beneath him like a bell, he circles the stage, his face flushed with wit or his chin drawn deep into his ruff in longing. Like many of Shakespeare's women, Olivia isn't the most scintillating character onstage – she's not a villain – but Rylance's work with Carroll adds layers of unspoken narrative to the text; he writes with his body. He's a play within a play unto himself.

SGT's all-male company worked in repertory with the remounted *Twelfth Night* and *Richard III*. The company in rep was so successful that they were able to secure funding and stage both productions on Broadway at the Belasco Theatre. New York Theatre critics such as Ben Brantley of the *New York Times* (10 November 2013) praised the productions whilst audiences flocked en masse to get a coveted ticket for these 'original practices' transplants:

> This 'Twelfth Night' – which opened on Sunday in repertory with a vibrant and shivery 'Richard III' that allows Mr. Rylance to show he's as brilliant in trousers as he is in a dress – makes you think, 'This is how Shakespeare was meant to be done'.

The 2013 production was nominated for seven Tony Awards, winning two – one for Mark Rylance's performance of Olivia in the best actor in a featured role category. In an on-camera interview with *Broadway World TV* (2014) following his Tony Award win, Rylance spoke about the production and its all-male dynamics:

> There's something also about a group of men working together on something they get very much into the craft of what they are doing and a lot of these men are now fathers too and so they are very ... quite a few gay men in the company too and then some younger men, single younger men. So the mixture of these fathers and gay men and younger men is a fascinating group to work with. I also like working with women, don't get me wrong, but there is a different dynamic when the genders work on their own. I wish there were more all-women companies. I've seen that happen and that's a very good thing too.

Certainly billing the productions an 'original practices' experiment gives the work an air of authority and authenticity that other single-sex performances, such as those by the all-women companies, find harder to claim. This may be one of the reasons behind *Twelfth Night's* success in both London and New York. Contributions by specialist and highly talented actors such as Mark Rylance may also carry a legitimising weight. Before his Tony win for *Twelfth Night*, Rylance had been celebrated by critics and audiences and had two previous Tony Award wins.

Whatever the recipe to success may be, it has also been shared by other successful all-male companies in the UK such as Cheek By Jowl, Propeller and the Lord Chamberlain's Men. The UK audiences' all-male appetite seems to have been whetted by SGT and has led to the formation and prosperity of these companies.

Propeller

The all-male company Propeller began in 1997 under the direction of Edward Hall, son of RSC founder and director Peter Hall. Despite the overwhelming reputation of his father, Edward Hall has carved out an outstanding directing career for himself through the auspices of the company. The company started with a production of *Henry V*, first performed in 1997 at the Watermill Theatre in Newbury England. Since that time, the company has toured internationally, has conducted educational and artistic workshops and has developed a long list of artists it has employed over the years. Previous productions include *The Taming of the Shrew*, *Twelfth Night*, *Richard III*, *Rose Rage* and *The Merchant of Venice*. The company is well respected and their productions have received many awards and accolades such as a New York Off Broadway 'Obie' award, Theatre Awards UK for best touring production, and best director, best design and best ensemble awards.

In addition to providing all-male Shakespeare as their primary format for productions, as expressed on their official website (2014), the company also aims to:

find a more engaging way of expressing Shakespeare and to more completely explore the relationship between text and performance. Mixing a rigorous approach to the text with a modern physical aesthetic, they have been influenced by mask work, animation and classic and modern film and music from all ages.

Propeller presents their works usually in repertory, and their performances are featured in residence at The Watermill Theatre or on tour internationally. They perform full-length productions, as well as their 'Pocket Shakespeare' project work, part of their education and outreach initiative.

The company has done remarkably well over the years and built a solid audience following. Many audience members follow the company as they tour and have become fans on Facebook and other social media formats. Critics, such as Petra Schofield for *Theatre Bath* (20 November 2013), have also praised the company, stating that:

This is a remarkable all male company who morph between ensemble and principal characters alike, the music is captivating and the direction of the company over the multi level set quite magical.

However, not all critics have continued to love the work, and in 2012, *The Telegraph* reviewer Dominic Cavendish alludes to their work as falling into cliché and needing a makeover. He indicates that he has followed the company's work for some time, but criticises the *Henry V* productions and a remounted *The Winter's Tale* as 'starting to stall and lose altitude?' Cavendish goes on to state:

> While the lusty commitment of this band of brothers isn't in doubt, the value of the project, in its current gender-biased form, perhaps is ... Hall brings newcomers into the mix with enough rejuvenating elan to ensure that Propeller has the air of a crack troupe rather than a motley crew – but having a certain momentum isn't the same as a raison d'etre. While the case for putting blokes in dresses – a throwback to Shakespeare's day – can be persuasively made when it comes to the histories and comedies in which confusion or sexual ambiguity runs rife, I didn't emerge from either of these productions feeling that the exclusion of actresses was especially useful; in many ways it's just distracting. (26 March 2012)

He also adds, 'It's often inventive, mischievous and efficient but it rather overdoses on its own testosterone' and swipes at their all-male convention suggesting that it may be 'Time for a rethink, chaps?'(2012).

On 2 May 2014 I held a personal interview with Dugald Bruce-Lockhart from Propeller. He has been working as an actor and director for the company for over 15 years taking part in 12 productions, including the recent touring production of A *Midsummer Night's Dream* (2013–2014). My aim for the interview was to discuss the company's history and performance approach, but also wanted to know more about his personal experiences playing cross-gender. What follows are extracts from that interview.

TP: Tell me about the history of the company.

DBL: I met Ed in Japan when I was with the Royal Shakespeare Company and he came to see the show, and I was introduced to him by another mate Tam Williams. Ed said, I got this idea about Henry the Fifth, and this was in 1996. We talked about it then, and then, two years later it happened ... I've been there from the start.

TP: Can you tell me about the originating ideas of the company? Why did Ed want to start a single-sex company?

DBL: It started out kind of by accident. From the first show, he had this idea of the chorus of Henry the Fifth, rather than being one person, being told by many. He always wanted to do an ensemble piece, and it occurred to him that if the chorus was made up of 15 squaddies then these squaddies provided an ensemble choric narrative structure that could then tell the story. Of course, I suppose, he could have had women too, but at the time he decided to do it all-male and with people he knew ... in a sense the all-male thing is kind of accidental.

During our interview he described the opening sequence of *Henry V* and explained that they used the concept of the soldiers being 'squaddies' that enter the playing space. As they enter, they find an old crown in an ammunition case and the playing structure begins to take shape.

> **DBL:** All the squaddies are like 'we are tired, knackered, thirsty, cold and hungry'.

The characters desired reflections on 'better days' and the idea was conceived of telling the play as an enacted story to entertain the bored characters. They used the 'found' props and costumes to dress their characters and created the story using very little other than the actors tools of voice, movement and imagination. This framing device created a story-within-a-story convention and allowed the actors to perform using a choral approach.

> **DBL:** He finds this crown and he starts with 'O for a muse of fire', remembering the old days when we were strong and the country was good and actually everybody picks up the idea 'should we tell a story? Yes, lets tell a story, let's pretend. So we say to the audience pretend that when you see one of us, you see a thousand, and imagine the horses. And as we did that we started to sing, old clothes came out of these boxes, and we said 'right you be Edie, you be Canterbury. No, I want to be Canterbury. You be the Dauphin!' So we had a complete organic storytelling mechanism and we literally dressed up as children would to tell a story.

The choral approach also gave the actors licence to play the female characters in the story, and their cross-gender choices were simple and suggestive rather than an embodied representation.

> **DBL:** Of course, because there were three female characters we had to dress up and play girls. In a sense, we treated those characters no different than any other character. Basically the chorus was telling the story and whatever character they had to play. We put on

a tiny bit of lipstick, and in Henry the Fifth it was more comedic, the roles are more comedic, even Kate at the end, but Mistress Quickly … just a little dress, just a bonnet, in the same way that the Dauphin would put on, maybe, a blue jacket. When the play finished the audience liked it so much that they said 'we want to see more of that'.

Discovering that they had created a unique convention for their all-male ensemble and storytelling, the company decided to do another production with a similar device. They produced *The Comedy of Errors* and then *Henry VI* (parts 1, 2 and 3) and then worked on *A Midsummer Night's Dream*.

> DBL: And each one had a choric ensemble identity. And we found that because the language was written with the ironies of the understanding that men are playing women, and in *Twelfth Night* you've got a man playing a girl playing a boy, all the resonances in the text really carry and have particular weight. On the one hand it stops that thing that can be really good about sexual chemistry on stage which something like *Romeo and Juliet* or some of the comedies like *Much Ado About Nothing* you really need. On the other hand, this allowed the audience to accept the device which allowed your imagination to do all the work. You realise that the stories are really about the human heart, not about the human skin or gender. It's about the heart and the heart can be male, female … it's irrelevant.

From our discussion, I sensed that the company received backlash as a result of being another all-male Shakespeare company, lacking roles and jobs for women. We discussed the all-male configuration of the company at length, and Lockhart expressed that the primary reason the company remained single-sexed was because their audiences demanded it. There was a point in their development process when they might have brought women into the ensemble and openly discussed doing so, but their audiences said,

> DBL: 'No. Don't. Because there are lots of companies that do that. This is different; so why not be different?' It had nothing to do with the fact that Shakespeare … originally he had to do that because he had no choice.

It is important to note that the decision to remain a single-sex male company was not, as in the SGT case, to recreate a 'historical'

Shakespearean theatre. Propeller's work is not focused on 'original practices' and does not utilise such references in the marketing of their shows. Their cross-gender actors are not trying to emulate the practice of a boy player or represent women in a naturalistic portrayal, but rather, they work towards pure storytelling and ensemble play through a choral convention.

Lockhart also discussed the benefits of working creatively in the single-sex environment, explaining that the all-male ensemble configuration creates a shorthand for creative practice. The result is that during the development and rehearsal process, the company spends far less time working to achieve results than when working with mixed casts. However, this shorthand process can also circumvent psychological layers, at the expense of discovering the deeper meaning found in the text, and the richer relationships between characters. Lockhart explains that there are times that they,

> DBL: ... lose some of the delicacy that you would get from a mixed cast. On the other hand, it allows us to be very robust physically in a way that we might not. The whole point is allowing the audience to do the work in their imagination, as you do when you read a book. We found that the formula works so at the moment we're not changing it. And more than that, we've been asked by theatres and our audiences not to change it.

Their robust physicality and choric convention are part of the unique signature of the company and serve to distinguish them from the other all-male Shakespeare companies in the UK. Unlike SGT's approach to performing cross-gender roles, Propeller leaves more to the imagination of the audience and never allows them to fully forget that the actors are an ensemble composed entirely of men. Even in feminine farthingales, suggestive headbands and lipstick – five o'clock shadows – hairy chests and well-defined biceps disrupt the gender illusion.

This approach may not have the immediate depth and legitimacy as the SGT company's performance, but it serves to illuminate gender performance and the text in new ways. For example, there may have been psychological layers missing from their approach to the *Taming of the Shrew*, but their unique choral convention and hyper-physicality electrified the stage and elevated the brutal conflict between Kate and Petruchio to epic proportions. Because of the layers of performativity in the play-within-the-play structure, Lockhart plays Christopher Sly in the prologue scenes before the first act, later transforming into Petruchio (I.ii).

The cross-gendered roles are clearly delineated as roles (we never forget they are men in female parts), and the 'taming' is rough and raw. Kate is powerful, bold, muscular, angry and, though smaller in stature than Petruchio, quite masculine – even in a dress. When she finally seems to submit to Petruchio in Act IV, the moment comes with a profound sense of defeat that is hard to swallow. It is a clear abandoning of will and is made more visible as we can see Kate's external strength in the body of a man and her breaking spirit not being related to lack of sleep or food but that of psychological abuse. The effect is that *Shrew* is interpreted differently than in a mixed cast, and its brutality is over-emphasised through meta-theatrical gender play. It in no way reads as a comedy by its conclusion.

Initially the company performed *The Taming of the Shrew* and *Twelfth Night* (2006) in repertory, and Lockhart played Petruchio and Olivia in the productions simultaneously. I wondered what such a unique experience, playing two genders in repertory, was like for him as an artist. I wondered what considerations and choices he made for both roles and how he negotiated between the characters' genders in two very different roles.

TP: Do you find it challenging to play across genders? You went from playing Petruchio to playing Olivia. Tell me about that experience.

DBL: I did enjoy it. I enjoyed my dress. I enjoyed the boots. I loved my dress. I had great fun with it and I would probably take on a role like that again but the difficulty I found with Olivia is that she is quite a heightened character anyway. She is a bit of a Diva … Of course one has to be careful because a man playing that sort of role you immediately get close to pantomime, close to cliché, close to the more traditional comedy.

TP: Like the Dame[2] characters?

DBL: Yes, exactly. Because she is like that; she has this Diva-ish-ness about her. Also this very vulnerable, excitable, delicate heart underneath it. I probably would, on hindsight, play something more along the lines of playing Kate or Beatrice, but actually I enjoy playing the men more, and some of the guys really enjoy playing the women. And the point is that none of them ever try to pretend to be female in any way whatsoever. Obviously you try to refine your movements so it's not too obvious all the time, but it's about not doing things that would make it stand out rather than trying to do things to (convince); because we are not going to convince the audience that we're women. That's not the point.

We are just trying to play the characters. What I found with Olivia is that because there is something about her in the language, in the way it was written, I found myself starting to move in a certain way and I thought I was betraying our ethos in the way we play women. I found that for me it was an interesting doubling with Petruchio certainly. And I think that because I was playing Petruchio who is so brutal, I probably went a little too far in the direction of, maybe as an actor, trying to show that I could be delicate and feminine. Which is not the point of playing the character. I had my good days and bad days, and looking back I would probably stick to playing men, but then there are some guys that would really really enjoy and would rather play the female roles.

TP: Can you outline for us what your company's ethos for playing female characters is?

DBL: The main thing is not to give the audience the impression that we are trying to convince you that we are women. The ethos is that you are looking at a character. And whether that character is a grandfather, an uncle, a daughter, a son, it's a character in a story and that's it.

This approach to playing the roles isn't unique to Propeller and could be applied to mixed gender casts. Indeed other Shakespeare companies, particularly ones dealing with gender imbalances in their casts, often use this convention in their productions of gender-swapped roles, such as the Judith Shakespeare Company's *Two Gentlemen of Verona* (2010). Lockhart has even used it in directing work with actors in order to free them from sex-typing and as a means to allow the performers to play more vigorously in the rehearsal process. Lockhart explains, the convention creates 'a game' for the actors and audiences, and for the single-sex companies, or companies experimenting with gender, in performance this gives them a shared dialogue and reference point for the playing. He states that such companies need:

DBL: … some sort of template in order to understand what the rules of the game are. The game in our company is that we are all men, so therefore we all play the characters. And in these stories are female and male characters, young and old. And it's no different from a 30 year-old playing a 60 year-old. You just accept it.

He then expresses that the approach they take is primarily to present the characters, not to embody them. They use a process that allows them not to focus on the gender of the character but relies heavily on an:

> DBL: ... understanding what the character wants, serving the text and paying, in a sense, no attention to the gender and paying more attention to the character.

However, as discussed in earlier chapters, most audiences are socialised to read and perform gender from birth. They bring gender expectations and stereotypes to the theatre when they attend a performance. Therefore they require visual cues from the actors in order to follow the storyline and to reread gender if cross-gendering is part of the playing. Here, the company takes pains to make suggestions of gender to aid the audience's imaginations. For example, in the company's *A Midsummer Night's Dream* (2013) when defining Hermia for an audience visually:

> DBL: You have to go for height, that's in the text, you go with her kind of dress that goes with her character. Helena calls her a maypole, so we have an outfit that suggests the maypole; a little bit of lipstick, perhaps, but they (the cast) all have lipstick. They are all slightly androgynous in the first place.

In performance, Propeller's work and its use of the ensemble, through physical playing, minimal setting and costume and the fusion of musical performance and choral singing, mark their work as quite Brechtian. And their approach to creating cross-gender and other characters can be described as 'Gestus'. When playing the female roles in the play there is a gestural physicality in the work that presents a theatrical femininity, rather than that of real women in the audience or of another period. He explains that:

> DBL: Those gestures are adopted because they help. A little attention is paid to that but it is never directed. That is up to the actor to research.

Lockhart also points out that there are pitfalls of playing cross-gender. The cross-gender actor is continually walking a tightrope between finding feminine theatrical gestures that work for the play and overplaying the gender performance so much that it disrupts the story. He believes Shakespeare has moments in which there is a knowing nod to the audience; when in a well-crafted moment we all recognise the gender play-within-the-play at work. However, he stresses that the focus must always be on the storytelling.

The Lord Chamberlain's Men

Another all-male touring company that is working on walking the line between storytelling and cross-gender play in the UK is the Lord Chamberlain's Men. Established in 2004, and borrowing their name from one of the playing companies that Shakespeare was known to have worked with, the Lord Chamberlain's Men are an all-male Shakespeare summer touring troupe that, as stated on their website, 'brings its unique blend of all male Shakespearean entertainment to only the most beautiful and historic open air venues, where the audiences can sit under the stars, sip a glass of wine and enjoy a picnic while being enthralled in true Elizabethan fashion' (2014).

Unlike Propeller, the Lord Chamberlain's Men aim to give audiences a taste of historical practice, evoking a sense of what it may have been like to have attended a Shakespeare play performed by Shakespeare's original travelling players. This ethos is embedded in their simple staging, all-male casting, costumes, set and prop design and touring schedule, reminiscent of Elizabethan theatre aesthetics and playing practices.

> The actor-musicians of the company follow the same principles that Shakespeare himself championed: clear, bold and dynamic storytelling in the open air, seasoned with a healthy dose of music, songs and comedy combine to make a Lord Chamberlain's Men production the perfect way to spend a summer's evening. (2014)

Not as prolific or as popular as SGT or Propeller, the Lord Chamberlain's Men have carved out a niche for themselves in the summer al fresco theatre market and have attracted audiences over the last decade. They have produced nine productions starting with a visually 'energetic' and 'exciting' Macbeth in 2004 that was remounted in 2012.

The troupe of touring actors is generally small which helps with transportation and accommodation costs and also allows the company to mirror what is argued as original practice for touring companies in the Elizabethan era. It is believed that Shakespeare's touring troupes would have consisted of no more than about seven to eight players. The limited cast number meant that the actors would have played all the characters (including the female roles), and double and, in some cases, triple castings of parts would have occurred (Thomson 1992, Gurr 2004). The troupes had a limited repertory of plays on tour that were simpler in their staging and setting, and these pieces were easily adapted to a variety of playing spaces, many of which were outdoor (Thomson 1992). Additionally, it is believed that shorter versions of the plays, sometimes produced in London and then remounted for touring, would have been performed.

In his book *Shakespeare by Stages* Arthur Kinney describes the limits and conditions of Elizabethan touring. He writes that the productions were 'largely void of sets and properties' and that the overall 'staging was traditionally minimal' (2003: 2). Stages found in the provinces were mostly open spaces with a curtain to signify that it was to be used as a playing space. Plays were also staged in a variety of non-theatrical sites such as 'marketplaces on market days' or perhaps 'open fields bordering villages', and performances were even held in spaces like a 'civic meeting room such as a courtroom' (2003: 2). Although the playing spaces were varied they had the following in common: 'their essential emptiness; they were bare platforms that were spatially neutral until the playwright himself defined them' (2003: 12).

The Lord Chamberlain's Men, like Shakespeare's company before them, find that altering their performances to suit different spaces quite challenging at times. But unlike Shakespeare's company, they also have to contend with modern expectations for theatrical performances, including that of effects and technological enhancements. In an interview for the *Lincolnshire Echo* (21 June 2012), Olly Pengelly discusses the challenges contemporary actors face when using Elizabethan practices in performance and on tour:

> Everywhere we go presents us with a new challenge because not only is every venue that we play very different vocally, also the surroundings are always very different. We haven't got the effects; it's not like in a theatre where we can use really clever lighting to create the atmosphere or anything like that.

The Lord Chamberlain's Men have included many of the original conditions in their contemporary practice as they tackle the challenge of touring and adjusting performances to varying sites and audiences. This is not always understood as part of their historical context approach by audiences and reviewers. For example, in Rebecca Tivey's *PlaytoSee.com* review of the 2012 remount of *Macbeth* she seems to criticise the simple set and the 'heavily edited' version of the play but finds great satisfaction in the cross-gender performance work of the men playing women, particularly noting that:

> Craig Ritchie is entirely believable as Lady Macbeth, capturing the sinister nature of her character through commanding presence and

delivery. It was interesting to see the character of Lady Macbeth without the typical seductive slant favoured by many female actors, and added a newly manipulative and threatening edge.

The company works to present female characters in a positive light and to give their audiences a sense of what it must have been like to watch a boy player in the role. However, despite the actors' care 'to recreate it seriously' and negotiate the 'fine line between a man in a dress being convincing or looking like a pantomime dame' by casting 'roles very carefully' (*Blast* 6 September 2006) at times the cross-gender performance falls short of the promise. Sheila Conner of the *British Theatre Guide* praised Andrew Young's portrayal of Titania in the company's 2006 *A Midsummer Night's Dream* writing that she enjoyed the character, 'not only appearing feminine but sounding so too', but found fault in the portrayals of Helena and Hermia by other actors. In her review of *Twelfth Night*, Lyn Gardner of *The Guardian* (9 August 2009) was even more critical of the cross-gender acting and overall approach:

> Andrew Normington's production is a good-natured affair that makes sensible cuts to accommodate the doubling made necessary by a cast of seven, and gives a straightforward, no-frills account of the text without really ever giving us the play. Unlike other all-male companies like Ed Hall's Propeller, these actors seldom seem comfortable with the cross-dressing or have the confidence to explore its erotic possibilities.

As this example illustrates, the challenges that are present in cross-gender performance are more complex than simply conveying a 'comfort' in playing the roles. The boy players and the playing of female roles in Elizabethan theatre were more poetic illusion rather than modern concepts of verisimilitude. Their presentation of 'women' was predominantly illusory and not representative of Elizabethan women, although the parts required an understanding of women's roles in society and certainly Shakespeare made commentary about this in the plays, the parts and the women's dialogue. As discussed earlier, *The Taming of the Shrew*, for example, gives a unique glimpse at some of the indoctrinating principles defining women's social roles, particularly as wife to a man of the times. The play has very different resonances today, as do our conceptions of gender and social rules.

For cross-gender performance to be successful there has to be a clear artistic approach, as in Propeller's Brechtian 'suggestion' of gender and roles or a well-trained methodological practice that may take time for the subtleties of the illusion to appear successfully to modern audiences. If we consider what Ronan Patterson describes as the difference between contemporary notions of 'boy players' and how Elizabethan boys were actually educated, prepared and trained to play females on stage, we can recognise a specialised difference. Rarely do male actors in the companies mentioned in this chapter 'train' to play female roles exclusively or even predominantly. Most have trained in acting schools to play a variety of roles and even for differing mediums. They have not specialised their study and training on cross-gender performance. If they have received training, this is mostly through encounters with specialist teachers and via workshops when working on a particular role or production.

This reference to a 'comfort level' with cross-gender performance in no way mirrors the breadth and depth of experience and training experienced by the Elizabethan boy players. To claim, in any way, that a contemporary practice is a copy of Elizabethan cross-gender practice lacks a contextual understanding of the period historically and in theatrical practice. It is also very suspect. However, as suggested earlier in this chapter, comparisons can be drawn between the Elizabethan boy players and that of the Japanese Onnagata performers. Such parallels are beautifully explored in the collaborative work of Minoru Fujita and Michael Shapiro (2006) and further discussions of both Elizabethan boy players and the Onnagata can be found in *The Changing Room* (2000) by Laurence Senelick. Contemporary practice in these all-male companies, thus far, has not produced this depth of training, education and apprenticeship. However, it is interesting to note that the all-female companies, discussed in the next chapter, seem to be building towards more methodological approaches to gender performance including company-specific training regimes and apprenticeships to aid women as they play male roles.

7
The Female Players and All-Female Companies

'Male classical actors might be better at playing men. But women are better at playing human beings... And Shakespeare is about human beings' (Rebecca Patterson, as quoted in *The Wall Street Journal* 22 April 2012). Influenced by the Commedia dell'arte troupes wherein women played both male and female roles in the 1660s, women began playing male roles on stage in England beginning in the Restoration period.[1] According to surviving records, one of the first male Shakespeare roles to be performed was that of Hamlet acted by Fanny Furnival at the Smock Alley Theatre in Dublin, 1741 (Howard 2009: 38). However, besides Howard's in-depth study of female Hamlets, very little documentation and scholarship has focused on this area of theatrical performance. Some historic performances are noted in a few resources, such as Charlotte Cushman's portrayal of Romeo in 1845, Sarah Siddons' Hamlet in 1775 and Sarah Bernhardt's 'manly' approach to Hamlet in 1899.[2] Despite a lack of records today, women performing as male Shakespeare characters was so prevalent in theatre that in 1911 *The New York Times* ran an article entitled 'Women in Male Roles: Long List of Prominent Actresses Who Have Yielded To That Ambition' (Anon, 1911) and in it the reporter writes:

> Since Siddons there have been more than fifty female Hamlets, many women Romeos and Shylocks, and Iagos and Richards. In fact, with the exception of Macbeth, Brutus, and Coriolanus, nearly every Shakespearean male character has been essayed by some actress.

Such presence of women in male roles was also discussed in an article published in the *Stratford Herald* on August 12, 1921. The reporter wrote

that 'A female Hamlet is not a novelty' but that 'a Shakespearean production played entirely by women is rare'. The article continued, giving
details about 'an interesting experiment' wherein a production of *King
Henry V* would be played by an all-female cast in the Memorial Theatre
in Stratford Upon Avon led by Marie Slade (1921 cited in Morris, 2012).

I find such articles astonishing to read as clearly many women have
played these iconic roles for centuries, and their history remains mostly
hidden or utterly lost. This is not to say that these performances were
successful. Indeed, if we are to believe *The New York Times* article, many
of these women's performances as male Shakespeare characters were a
'lamentable failure'. Failure or not, these women were the predecessors
of today's 'Female Players'.

In Japan, there is a more recent history of young women training and playing male roles for musical revue productions. Known as
otokoyaku or girl player, these performers and their highly convention-
alised performances have flourished since the early 1900s when the
Takarazuka Revue was first opened in Takarazuka, Japan by Kobayashi
Ichizo (Robertson 1998). In the West however, such cross-dressed performances of women performing in male roles, even in productions of
Shakespeare, were slowly eradicated from popular theatre. One reason
for this change in popular taste may have been the influence of natural-
ism in the theatre and audience's expectations of seeing 'real life' on
its stages as opposed to the emblematic non-naturalist genre presented
by cross-gender casting and traditional Shakespeare performance.
Certainly most productions of Shakespeare's plays were cast to adhere to
more realism standards; men played male roles, women played female
roles and many actors were type-cast according to their age, look and
even race.[3]

Whatever the cause for the decline in the convention, it is obvious
that there was a clear move away from the popularity and prevalence
of women playing male roles in Shakespeare productions from the
early 1900s until about the 1990s when gender studies in universities
and all-female Shakespeare companies began to surface, particularly in
the US. In her book *Women Direct Shakespeare in America* (2005) Nancy
Taylor suggests that women's increasing presence in Shakespeare productions during this time period may be a result of the 'flourishing
women's movement' (2005: 27) of the 1970s and because 'women were
hired as artistic directors for a number of American regional theatres'
(2005: 28) in the subsequent decade. Director Phyllida Lloyd agrees that
women in key positions of power in the theatre certainly help to get
women's work produced but that, in the UK, such opportunities were

not readily accepted. She explains that the fault of her generation of women was that when offered such positions of power, particularly in the 1980s, arts funding was cut and many women 'ran in fear away to freelance careers' because they did not know 'how you can run a building that is completely underfunded and direct plays at the same time' (Gompertz 2012). This may explain the large difference in the numbers of all-female and female-led Shakespeare companies between the two countries operating today.

Whatever the reason for the difference in proliferation of such companies between countries, it is evident that the women's movement had direct influence on the development of female-driven Shakespeare Companies in North America. One notable US-based artistic collaboration from this period was co-directed by psychologist Carol Gilligan and voice expert Kirstin Linklater. Their gender studies class held in 1990 at Emerson College in Boston quickly became the springboard for the first all-female Shakespeare company of the period, aptly named Company of Women. The company's mission was to create Shakespeare productions that were 'performed, informed and transformed by multi-cultural, multi-generational all-women casts while developing original dramatic material and conducting workshops strengthening the voices of women and girls' (Company's *King Lear* Programme 1996). Interestingly, this mission statement is echoed in the statements of several all-female Shakespeare companies that sprouted in America not long after the Company of Women was founded and began producing shows and workshops. For example, the Los Angeles Women's Shakespeare Company, founded in 1993, declares that its aim is to create:

> professional productions of Shakespeare's plays with an all-female ensemble. We provide opportunities for collaboration between multiracial, highly accomplished artists who are actors, producers, directors, choreographers, designers and educators. (LAWSC website 2010)

Another company with a similar mission was *Woman's Will* founded in 1998 by Erin Merritt in San Francisco. The company, now no longer running due to loss of funding, aimed to:

> provide opportunities for women and girls to work together in a supportive yet challenging environment, to entertain and educate through high quality classes and performances, and to expand the boundaries in which audiences and artists see themselves. (Women's Will website 2010)

The company also shared the aim to promote diversity in casting and audience accessibility, explaining on their website (2010) that:

> Woman's Will is a multi-ethnic company that operates under a strict policy of non-discrimination and strives for triple accessibility at every event: all people must be able to reach our events, afford our events, and relate to our events.

In fact, a quick survey of these American all-female or female-focused Shakespeare companies (including the Queen's Company, the Judith Shakespeare Company and Chickspeare) reveals striking similarities in their missions and clear feminist viewpoints. Nearly all of the companies strive to promote women's participation in theatre, to achieve diversity in casting, to challenge audience's preconceived notions of gender and to include young girls in theatre-making. All of these companies were founded in the US, and there have been few records of any professional all-female Shakespeare companies currently operating or being founded in other English-speaking nations.[4] Nancy Taylor may hold the answer here as she writes that American female Shakespeare directors receive 'less critical attention' as America is a multifarious culture that embraces a 'less formal approach to Shakespearean productions' (2005: 28) than perhaps the traditionalist UK.

This is not to say that other English-speaking nations, including England itself, are so reverent of Shakespeare that they cannot accept an all-female cast performing these classical works. Cross-gender castings of Shakespeare's plays have been staged in England and other English-speaking countries for centuries. Recent notable explorations with all-female casts have been produced by such companies and in such sites as SGT, Smooth Faced Gentlemen, the Hartwell Players, Toronto Workshop Productions Theatre, Theatre Passe Muraille, Classic Chic and the Sydney Opera House, all of which operate outside of the US. In England, there have been notable contemporary performances by leading female actors in male Shakespeare roles such as Kathryn Hunter's portrayal of the title roles of King Lear and Richard III, Fiona Shaw's cross-gendered performance of Richard II at the National Theatre, Janet McTeer's Petruchio and Vanessa Redgrave's Prospero at SGT. Let's not forget Lloyd's all-female *Julius Caesar* at the Donmar Warehouse and the upcoming *Hamlet* with Maxine Peake in the title role at the Manchester Royal Exchange (2014).

Despite these shimmering and brave performances, the critical response to the UK productions provides an interesting comment as to the perceived reception and validity of such artistic endeavours and emphasises the critical markers of successful and disappointing cross-gender performance attempts. Amongst the more critically disappointing performances was Fiona Shaw's turn in *Richard II* directed by Deborah Warner at the National Theatre in 1995. Shaw's performance, though commanding and noteworthy in theatre history, may have been met with such scepticism and condemnation by the critics, because it challenged notions of gender and performance in Shakespeare country. It may also have been a reaction to the vague approach Shaw took with the playing of her character's gender. Shaw herself later explained in her *Salon* interview (15 February 1996) that she 'had no intention of playing a man' and instead was portraying King Richard II as 'somebody who perceives himself to be a non-man'.

Shaw's comments might seem to be a kind of justification for what was, for her, a disappointing performance of a male character, but the very fact that she played this character was in itself 'an experiment' for both Shaw and the theatre community. Although her performance lacked critical acclaim, it was a serious attempt at portraying masculinity through cross-gender casting and a full-bodied and psychological exploration, Shaw's performance inspired other female actors to explore such possibilities in very public performances in England and abroad.

Not long after Shaw's cross-gender performance, another British female actor attempted to play a cross-gender Shakespeare character on the professional stage. Kathryn Hunter played the title role in Shakespeare's *King Lear* at the Leicester Haymarket Theatre in 1997. The media has since billed her as 'The First British Actress to Play King Lear' but given the number of women playing male roles up until 1911 in America, as suggested by the previously mentioned *New York Times* article, I find it hard to believe that Hunter is the first woman in British history to step into this part. However, Hunter can be considered the first contemporary female actor to play the role professionally and her performance should be noted as the first in a prolific line of cross-gender roles that she would subsequently perform.

In her 'playing' of Lear, Hunter approached the role much like Shaw approached Richard II, as an androgynous character. This portrayal, much like Shaw's, generated some heated criticism as a 'meaningless exercise in modish casting' (*Daily Telegraph* 1 March 1997). However, perhaps warming to the convention, many of Hunter's critics also praised her efforts. Elizabeth Klett (2005: 58) notes they found that 'The greatness of Hunter's performance' was that, according to these reviews, it 'allowed gender to disappear'.

Perhaps encouraged by this positive criticism, Hunter went on to play such cross-gender roles as Richard III at SGT (2003), Dr James Barry in *Whistling Psyche* at the Almeida Theatre (2004), the male lead in *The Bee* at the Soho Theatre (2006) and the Fool in *King Lear* at the RSC (2010). Even Hunter's portrayal of *Celestina* at the King's Theatre in Edinburgh (2004) is worth noting. Although she played the title role, which is a female character, Hunter's portrayal was uniquely masculine as she wore a suit, smoked a cigar, had shaved her head and embodied a variety of male 'mannerisms'. Ksenija Horvat from *The Edinburgh Guide* (19 August 2004) noted, 'When she limps across the stage it is with the mobster's swagger, and her smooth-talking tongue pours poison in everyone's ears with an ease of the snake of Eden'. In nearly every review, whether positive or negative, Hunter's performance was noted as being exceptional. For example, critic Lynne Walker of the *Independent* (2004) gave the production only one star and called the production event 'a remarkably unsatisfying evening' but also noted, 'The show does have the great advantage of a brilliant central performance by Kathryn Hunter.'

Watching Hunter's work on stage in such roles and reading the countless reviews on her cross-gender performances reveal two very interesting qualities that I believe are the reason her performances in such roles, above all other female actors attempting the convention, bears such recognition. Hunter, despite her diminutive stature, continually practises 'shape-changing tours de force' (*The Observer* 21 August 2004) in performance. Her physical prowess is foregrounded in nearly every one of her roles as she draws upon her years of experience and training using her physical body to shape-shift into any character she plays including male roles. Speaking about her physical performance of playing Richard III at SGT in an interview for *What's On Stage* (23 June 2003), she explains that playing the character is a very physical process:

> He does have very high testosterone – he likes to fight and loves war, he's quite macho. So I have to keep checking that I'm not thinking like a woman and instead attend to that mentality. You look at the mentality and then translate that into physical action.

Indeed Hunter's Richard III (2003) was a highly physicalised embodiment and the critics did not miss the chance to praise the overall effect of her approach:

> her portrayal of Richard is amazing. Barely five feet tall – her physique twisted, her chest thrust forward, one leg permanently stiff

with pointed toe, her right arm seemingly withered – she jerks across the stage like the 'bottled spider' Richard is cruelly described as. Think one of film maker David Lynch's sinister dwarfs, but instead of repelling she seems magnetic, sexual and very, very intelligent. (*Curtainup* 2003)

The critics also discuss her cross-gender performance commenting that 'the pose she strikes caricatures a dashing gent' (*The Independent on Sunday*), 'you entirely forget that she is a woman playing a man' (*The Times*) and that because of her successful cross-dressed performance, Hunter 'goes some way to justifying the theatre's claim, which is (a) some actresses merit a go at the big classical roles, and (b) audiences relish having their imaginations stretched and stretched' (*The Times*).

Indeed, Hunter's highly physical performance was so remarkable that it is discussed in over a dozen reviews published on the production. Equally remarkable is the number of reviewers that draw parallels between Hunter's performance of Richard and the historic portrayal by Anthony Sher for the RSC in 1984 that won him a Lawrence Olivier Award. In his glowing review of Hunter's performance for *The Times*, Nightingale draws an interesting comparison between the two performances and states, 'If you want a Richard who combines glee and wit with physical invention, Sher was your man and Hunter is your woman' (*The Times*).

Although there are a plethora of positive reviews, especially in reference to Hunter's physical embodiment of the role, there are some negative reviews and, in fact, most critics found the vocal aspects of Hunter's performance quite lacking. At times the critics are rather vicious in their criticisms of Hunter's voice: 'her husky voice has something of the caw about it' (*The Daily Telegraph*), 'when she lowers her voice, she is almost inaudible' (*The Sunday Times*), 'sometimes hard to hear' (*The Evening Standard*), 'her voice is alarmingly limited in its range' (*The Daily Telegraph*), and it is not just the sound or quality of her voice that is under attack in these reviews. Several critics also comment on what they consider Hunter's lack of training in performing Shakespeare's text vocally, suggesting that she pays more attention to the physicality of the role and not the linguistic craftsmanship embedded in all of Shakespeare's plays. John Gross complained, 'when it comes to talking her lines, she is hopeless. She shortens them and robs them of colour; it is as though she were doing her best to turn Shakespeare into prose' (*The Sunday Telegraph*). John Peter noted, 'She has a lordly way with the lines, pausing on the wrong beat, missing the rhythm, stressing the wrong words' (*The Sunday Times*).

Studying Shaw and Hunter's cross-gender performances reveals some key points of consideration that are clearly intrinsic to generating a successful attempt at playing male roles. Firstly, a female actor playing a male role must make a very clear choice in regard to their gender performance in the production. To play 'androgyne' or 'non-man' as a gender creates a vague effect that serves only to further disrupt the acting and the artistic vision already complicated by the imposed cross-gender casting. However, it is interesting to note that in Hunter's portrayal of Celestina, her bold choice of performing a female character as very masculine resulted in a critically successful performance. Secondly, when a female actor plays a male role she must be fully prepared to physically embody the character. Without a fully embodied performance of masculinity, the female actor exposes her 'natural' gender which can disrupt the effect of the performance and awaken an audience from the 'suspension of disbelief', marking the performance as unsuccessful. Indeed, Yolanda Vasquez from the SGT 2003 *The Taming of the Shrew* discusses the all-female cast's discovery of the physical demands of playing male roles: 'we realized … the amount of energy needed, physical energy, to be these men … was exhausting' (Carson and Karim-Cooper 2008: 202). The physicality of such roles cannot be ignored as audiences and critics scorn a half-hearted attempt to realise the strength, power and physical prowess demanded by these roles. The most scathing remarks in the reviews of SGT's *Richard III* (2003) relate to the most physical moments in the play – the fight scenes and battles. It is in these moments on stage that the critics claim the production resembles 'a girls' school play' (*The Independent*) and 'a playground bout of Grandmother's Footsteps' (*The Independent on Sunday*) and sneer that 'a hen-night with handbags would be more exciting' (*The Daily Telegraph*).

Finally, the last point of consideration for a successful cross-gender performance, particularly in Shakespeare plays, is a diligent attention to the voice and voicework.[5] Here is where process and product must meet the expectations of the audience and critics. Shakespeare's theatre is a performance of words, articulation, rhythm, language, structure and story. If an actor's vocal instrument is not highly tuned and fully developed to handle the vocal performance demands of Shakespeare's text, then the whole performance convention falls disastrously flat. Shakespeare's audiences still arrive at the theatre ready to 'hear' (*audire*) a play as opposed to being spectators (*spectre*) attending to 'see' a play. The vocal precision and performance of gender will be critiqued especially in cross-gender castings.

Attention to the voice, its vocal development, delivery and trans-formation to 'masculine' gender placements and pitches in the per-formances of women playing male Shakespeare roles is essential to a successful cross-gender performance. These considerations are all being addressed to various degrees by the all-female Shakespeare companies featured in this chapter.

The Los Angeles Women's Shakespeare Company

'I dreamed there was a company, all Female / Our joy was poetry, and lit this little town, Los Angeles / With radiant fire from our collective souls / Our unique cause challenged the world / We spoke in harmony as all the tuned spheres / And we were friends... / Think you there was or might be such a company / As this I dreamed of...?' (Wolpe's Melville award speech, 2014). The Los Angeles Women's Shakespeare Company (LAWSC) was founded in 1993 by actor/director Lisa Wolpe with the aim 'to produce professional productions of Shakespeare's plays with an all-female ensemble' (LAWSC website 2014). The company is one of the first and longest surviving all-female Shakespeare institutions in the US and can be cited as one of the most influential. It is estimated that over 1,000 women and girls have participated in LAWSC produc-tions and workshops (Avila 2014) and the company has links to other all-female companies and productions, such as those featured in this chapter. When American all-female companies discuss their influences, Lisa Wolpe and LAWSC are often mentioned.

Wolpe began the company with a view to expanding upon the pro-found work started by Gillian, Linklater and the Women's Company in the 1990s. Founded in multicultural Los Angeles, the company created collaborations between multiracial and interdisciplinary artists, provid-ing 'positive role models for women and girls' (LAWSC website 2014) and is one of the most prolific all-female companies in history, produc-ing over 15 Shakespeare plays spanning two decades.

Despite winning a bevy of awards, including the Los Angeles Critic Circle Margaret Hanford Award for Sustained Excellence in 2008 and the Lee Melville Award in 2014, the company has been primarily a labour of love for artistic director Wolpe. Struggling to produce one show a year the company primarily runs productions in small theatre spaces such as Hollywood's Actors Theatre, Miles Memorial Playhouse, the Boston Court Theatre in Pasadena and the Odyssey Theatre but has branched out into larger spaces in its history when it received vital funding. Although the company endeavours to 'pay modest stipends to our artists and staff' LAWSC operates primarily as 'a volunteer-based, grass-roots company with an enthusiastic and dedicated ever-expanding audience' (2014).

This fact is astonishing considering the prolific work and accomplished artists that have been involved since its inception. In addition to producing the work of Shakespeare with an all-female ensemble of actors, the company also employed women in roles offstage as well, including as producers, directors, administrators, choreographers, master teachers and designers:

> The sets, costumes and lights are designed and constructed by an all-female crew, and the administrative, producing, house management, box office, and backstage team is also all-female. We have also employed dozens of kids in our productions, and the girls and women become role models to one another as they work through the delights and mysteries of putting on a play together. (*Footlights* 31 July 2011)

In addition to creating roles for women, the company also embodied a multicultural ethos in its values, working hard to create collaborations that gave women of diverse backgrounds the chance to take leading roles in professional productions. One such collaboration started in 1993 when Wolpe and Natsuko Ohama worked together on LAWSC's inaugural production of *Romeo and Juliet*. Ohama played Friar Lawrence in the production and has remained a theatrical collaborator and Wolpe's 'master teacher for voice' for over three decades even co-directing *Hamlet* and sharing the lead role in 1995 (*LA Stage Times* 28 August 2013).

Primarily known for producing works of Shakespeare, the company has also staged productions from other playwrights including Oscar Wilde, a five-week festival of student work, original plays and adaptions. In the case of the five-week festival entitled 'Wicked Wilde Shakespeare Festival' in 2010, Wolpe created the project when she lost core funding for a production of *Richard II* she was developing with Timothy Douglas (*LA Stage Times* 26 May 2010). Such struggles to secure funding in Los Angeles for LAWSC projects seemed to wear Wolpe thin at times:

> I have to say that it's very hard and very disappointing being an artist in this economic climate ... Sometimes it feels like the end of the road. I see that others are figuring it out. I could tell people

I'm experimenting with new media or doing a play on Facebook but if people don't come to this, I'll lose my shirt. It's all on my credit card. (2010)

In earlier years, the company seemed to strive and they were able to procure funding from prestigious benefactors such as the California Arts Council, National Endowment for the Arts and the Arco Foundation. In 2000, LAWSC was even able to break away from its routine 99-seat Equity Waiver status and produced *Twelfth Night* in the 1200-seat John Anson Ford Amphitheatre with full Equity status. These financial successes aside, Wolpe admits it has always been a labour of love as she alone has been seeking funding, producing, directing and not being able to pay herself for that effort. She has had to take other work around the world in order to make a living and returns to Los Angeles with 'a big credit card bill' (*Footlights* 2012).

Add to this fact that there is a distinct funding crisis and companies such as LAWSC that once received funding are no longer securing those means. In the 2012 interview with Moore, Wolpe pointed out that funding for theatre projects was reduced by 40% and she spoke fatalistically about the company's future in *Curve* magazine (20 June 2012) comparing herself to the other struggling all-female Shakespeare companies that have been, or are on the verge of, folding. 'My company might fold this year, too ... No matter how fabulous we are we're not getting the funding that everyone else is getting. There are certainly more gay men succeeding in theater than gay women.'

That isn't to say that all the women that have participated in LAWSC or in this area of cross-gender practice are lesbian. On the contrary, the women are diverse and many are married to men and raising families at the same time that they are trying to forge a living from this art. The LAWSC artists work to achieve legitimacy in their practice and this usually begins with gender workshops and consciousness-raising sessions that help to empower the women and allow them to inhabit authoritative roles and move away from roles of victim and voicelessness.

In most of their productions LAWSC actors inhabit a 'renaissance' masculinity and do so through detailed studies of voice, movement and psychological realism. The costumes aid the transition from female-bodied actors to male Shakespeare roles, and many of the women wear beards and moustaches to hide their feminine features. However, the emphasis of the practice is less on the external 'habits' of the cross-gendered character and more on the internal process of discovery. Lisa Wolpe (Avila 2014) describes how she approaches this process:

> Playing Shakespeare's great roles is an alchemical process about unpacking the vulnerability of a villain or a man in order to understand why men do what they do. I am poised between victim and villain, comparing without despair, having a kind of perspective on both. To do that, I have to build a bridge between my own vulnerability as a female victim of various kinds of behavior (like being molested, or being physically hurt or frightened, being paid less as a grown-up and an artist than other people, or being confronted with a glass ceiling). I have to flip the story – inhabit my vision of being strong and capable and a person of potential, walk my talk.

Although many of the actors in LAWSC are given positive attention by audiences and critics for their performances, Lisa Wolpe generally receives the lion's share of critical praise for her mercurial transformations. Performing in *Othello* at the Boston Court (2008), Wolpe created an Iago that was a 'riveting portrayal ... believable as both a man and a character' (*Pasadena Weekly* 20 March 2008) and 'delightfully human' (*Talkin' Broadway* 28 February 2008) and her cross-dressed, highly realistic portrayal overshadowed others in the cast. Monji of *Pasadena Weekly* writes, 'Wolpe's Iago is fiercer than Fran Bennett's stiffly proud Othello' and 'Aarn's Cassio is noble, but doesn't seem a leader of men' (2008). Perlmutter of *Talkin' Broadway* also notes differences in the acting performances in her review of Othello:

> Linda Bisesti is posturing as a man in the role of Roderigo, but Wolpe's Iago actually is male. It isn't about a swagger or a lowering of voice. Just watching the way Iago sits and holds his cigarette tells you not only that he's a man, but a man of a certain class (not that high), a man of a certain attitude (that the world should give him what he believes is his due), and a man of thoughtfulness. (2008)

In 2011 Perlmutter opened her review of LAWSC's *Richard III*, in which Wolpe played the title role, with this declaration:

> As a rule, if you have an opportunity to see Lisa Wolpe in a Shakespeare play, you should take it. As a corollary, because Wolpe is so talented,

you should expect that the rest of the cast will not be up to her level. (*Talkin' Broadway* 12 September 2011)

Wolpe has years of experience that she brings to her roles and works hard to share her acting practice and cross-gender approach with other, sometimes younger, actors. The 2011 production of *Richard III* was staged as part of a university (Cal Poly Pomona) Shakespeare Festival and featured many student actors amongst the LAWSC equity actors. Although Wolpe focuses on creating opportunities in classical theatre for women, she doesn't leave men out of her practice and many male actors have benefitted from her knowledge and experience as well. In 2014 Wolpe directed a gender-swapped production of *The Revenger's Tragedy* cast with students from University of California Los Angeles' (UCLA) Theatre Department. The effect was enlightening as the male actors, stepping into the female roles, were forced 'to deal with having short scenes with few lines and underdeveloped personalities' (*Daily Bruin* 11 December 2014).

The company does more than produce plays and create expanded roles for women on and offstage. It serves a greater purpose in the community, which by and large, glances over women and minorities in the arts. The company has also facilitated educational outreach programmes, and these have made a great impact on the minds and talents of next generation artists. LAWSC's influence is immeasurable and far-reaching. Wolpe is more than just an artist; she is an activist and single-handedly tours the globe conducting workshops on cross-gender Shakespeare, directing productions for respected companies and repertory theatres, helping them to reconsider how gender is cast and staged in their productions.

Consider that in addition to directing at UCLA in 2014, Wolpe led workshops and performed as Iago in an all-female reading of Othello at the Harlem Shakespeare Festival, directed *The Winter's Tale* in Vancouver for an emerging all-female Shakespeare company, Classic Chic, and toured her solo production *Shakespeare and the Alchemy of Gender* internationally – including a performance at the Oregon Shakespeare Festival. Wolpe extends her reach not only through LAWSC performances but also in the many associations, performances and events she participates in. The impact is that in the theatre, 'women are being given the opportunities to rise, or are simply making their own progress, regardless of the difficulties' they continue to face (Avila 2014). Many women, particularly in Shakespeare performance, follow Wolpe's lead, reconsidering gender casting to create their own projects and all-female companies.

The Queen's Company

The Queen's Company is an all-female ethnically diverse company that was founded by artistic director Rebecca Patterson in 2000 and is based in New York City. Playing in Off-Off Broadway theatre spaces, the company is dedicated to providing opportunities for minority women in:

> top notch classical productions that breathe new life into the great plays with an attention to speaking the text beautifully combined with theatrical playfulness, while letting women have a go at playing the roles that boys have been hogging to themselves. (*New York Cool* 2005)

The Queen's Company has produced many critically acclaimed performances such as *School for Scandal, Anthony and Cleopatra, Edward II* and *Much Ado About Nothing* and the company's professional associations include Mark Rylance, SGT and Kathryn Hunter. On their board of directors is transgender theorist and performer Kate Bornstein. Kate serves as an advisor to many aspects of the company's practices including staging and performing cross gender and transgender roles and stories. In addition to the diversity, opportunity and vision the company provides, I also find its admitted Drag King, transgender and Asian influences interesting applications for cross-gender performance.

The Queen's Company's ties to Drag King and transgender communities are not easy to clearly trace. However, Patterson does speak about how such communities have influenced her practice and vision as a director. In a joint interview with disputed Drag King 'founder' Diane Torr in *The Brooklyn Rail* (1 September 2004), Patterson explains her viewpoint and distinctive interest in the area:

> I got started out looking at transgender performance, not necessarily drag performance, although I'm a huge admirer of it. Drag obviously is performing gender and accentuating gender, and I was more interested in what Kate Bornstein talks about, which is removing the filter of gender from performance, especially classical performances. The great classical roles inhabit both the male and the female. I wanted to appropriate traditionally male roles for female performers, to show that the entire range of human experience is apropos for a female performer.

Patterson continues to explain how she believes that transgender, as a performance convention, can be used to create a theatrical experience wherein cross-dressed characters (i.e. women playing men) might high-light, for an audience, a greater 'human experience' or rather a univer-sality of experience:

> Something I truly love about doing a play with transgender perfor-mance in it, is that you're telling a story with elements of love and elements of family in it. It's not simply our identity and our gender, but it's relationships within that. (2004)

What I find interesting in Patterson's viewpoint is that she terms cross-gender performance as 'Transgender' performance, borrowing such ideas from Kate Bornstein, and is able to argue that such performances present a universality of human experience. Indeed, this philosophy is espoused in company interviews and literature, and previously on the front page of their website, which proclaimed 'The mythic journey is a human journey that embraces the male and female in all of us' (Queen's Company website 2014).

Her use of what she calls Asian influences on the company's prac-tices and performances are also defined in such 'universal' terms. Again, not easily traced, these influences are most noticeable in the 'barefoot' approach to all the performances. This aesthetic was noted during a question-and-answer session the company held after a performance of *The Taming of the Shrew* at the Walker Space on 13 November 2005:

Question from audience member: Why are the characters barefoot?

Patterson: The Company's actors always perform barefoot. We use Asian and modern influences in all our productions. The act of being barefoot grounds the actor and provides unlimited choices. Shoes limit and dictate how an actor moves. This is our art and being bare-foot allows the art to occur, leaping over the 'realism' or 'idealism' and reminds the audience of the basic humanity of the actor.[6]

I worked directly with the company in 2005 on a production of *The Taming of the Shrew* and was able to observe their practices first-hand. Since that time I have been following the company as it has grown and produced major works, not only that of Shakespeare. Patterson's direction has a very robust and clear style that has been maintained since their origins. Many of the actors that first worked with the company have retained their presence in their productions over the last decade. Others have filtered in and out as their careers progress but still view the experiences of working with the company as expansive and, much like Cush Jumbo from Lloyd's *Julius Caesar* found the cross-gender experience, 'eye opening'.

When new actor 'newbies' work with the company they are invited to a training session wherein they are introduced to gender performance theory through a workshop format. Through this workshop the women discuss gender and how gender programming affects and effect them as women. They also look at 'gendered' behaviour and discuss how they might better prepare themselves for the performance at hand. For some this can mean examining their own gender performance as women and, if playing female characters, adhering to gender rules and/or amplifying feminine gestures and behaviours. For others playing male roles, this investigation period allows them to review their gender presentation and find more neutral modes of performing and then layering on masculine gender behaviours or signifiers, such as taking more space, being more physically assertive, or lowering their vocal register. These workshops help the women to explore the performance of gender before they have to begin the detailed task of exploring the character, context and narrative demanded by the play.

The effect is that they produce invigorating, physical and entertaining works that allow audiences to forget that they are a company of all women. The work is highly stylised, and unlike LAWSC's 'Renaissance' aesthetic, the Asian and contemporary influences make the productions feel classically fresh and alive. The women are highly trained actors, graduates from esteemed performance schools, and bring a plethora of specialist skills to their roles, including singing, dancing, playing instruments and sword fighting.

In 2005 when I joined the company their motto on the website was bold, declarative and confrontationally feminist: 'All Female. All the Time. No Apologies.' Since that time, the company seems to have softened its approach from an 'in-yer-face boys' position, to becoming a legitimate theatrical mainstay for New York women in classical theatre. The reviews and amount of positive press their productions receive are astounding, and a testament to the perseverance and dedication of not only Rebecca Patterson, but all the women significantly involved. However, the company still struggles to attract the funding it needs to significantly employ women in the theatre and, like many other all-female and women-focused companies, is reduced to producing one to two shows a year and generally paying artists at 'showcase' rates, if at all.

This discrepancy between the male companies and cross-gender opportunities and that of female companies and opportunities was the topic of a NY Equity Arts Council Panel in 2011. The panel was the brainchild of Gail Schaefer, a professional NY actor that served on the Equal Opportunity panel for the American Equity Association. Schaefer queried the panel when she realised that although they had many events for most minority groups, a 'women's history' day or event wasn't recognised. Schaefer then set up the panel to address the issue of women playing in male roles and to question why there wasn't as much opportunity for women particularly as this was a more prevalent practice for men to play women at the time:

> She actually went through the Equity casting roles and wrote down how many calls there were for women to play men, and how many for men to play women. At that time they were casting a lot of Ednas for *Hairspray* and they also had just done *The Importance of Being Ernest* with Brian Bedford. So suddenly there were all these men in drag everywhere and she said 'where are the women in drag? Why is this not happening?'[7]

Addressing the issue, Schaefer held an Equity panel discussion entitled 'Limitless Casting: Could the Best Man for the Part Be a Woman?' and invited several experts to attend and contribute to the discussion. Amongst the invitees were Rebecca Patterson of the Queen's Company, Joanne Zipay of the Judith Shakespeare Company and theatre scholar Richard Schechner. In my interview with Zipay (2014) she spoke passionately about the panel and how it was a landmark moment for Equity and a real honour for the companies and artists that were represented. She also discussed how Schechner contributed to the debate from a wider viewpoint and stated that he was clearly disappointed with the lack of women's opportunities to play male roles in the theatre.

> Richard Schechner talked about cultural movements and how he was very disappointed he said films should be behind theatre in things like this. Theatre should be always pushing the envelop on that stuff and he said theatre was behind. We are seeing a lot more gender chances taken in film than on stage. (Zipay 2014)

As a result of the panel discussion several of the companies and artists wanted to demonstrate through practice how women playing male roles was being addressed in a multitude of approaches. Three theatre companies, including the Judith Shakespeare Company and the Queen's Company, staged work for a follow-on panel workshop in 2013.

We did a series of scenes with cross-gender casting in a variety of different ways because each of our theatre companies has a different approach to it … Gail is really trying to continue to raise awareness of this type of casting. (Zipay 2014)

Chickspeare

Although these women and their companies appear predominately in major cities, such as New York and Los Angeles, that's not always the case. Smaller companies outside major metropolises are springing forth in greater numbers than in past decades. For example, in Charlotte, North Carolina, a small company was formed in 1998 called Chickspeare. Chickspeare began as a very innovative 'free for all' in a local brewery that would allow some sparky ladies to play all the roles in a Shakespeare play and despite the fact that the brewery 'sold its space in 2002' (Chickspeare website 2014), the company continued to produce work despite being 'bounced around numerous venues' (*Creative Loafing Charlotte* 18 December 2013) and even taking a hiatus for a few years.

The company was originally founded by Sheila Snow Proctor, Anne Lambert, Lolly Foy and Katie Oates and continues to thrive. Joanna Gerdy joined the company during their first production of *As You Like It*. At its inception, the company aimed 'to give women the opportunity to explore characters not otherwise available to them in most modern productions of Shakespeare's work … Chickspeare's goals are: to engage the audience with Shakespeare and provide a creative, provocative environment for female actors to explore and experience his plays'.[8]

Like similar fledgling professional Shakespeare companies fighting to endure over time, many of Chickspeare's original members 'went on to other projects, companies, or moved to other states' (Proctor 2014). Sheila Snow Proctor now runs the company as executive director and Joanna Gerdy as the artistic director. Over the last fifteen years the company has produced a number of productions such as *Macbeth*, *Julius Caesar* and *Twelfth Night*, gaining attention as being Charlotte, North Carolina's 'First and Only All Female Shakespeare Company' a distinction they proudly share on their website and social media sites. In addition to Shakespeare productions they have also presented plays from female playwrights like Maria Irene Fornas and Paula Vogel, as well as being drawn to 'other original works featuring all-female casts' (Proctor 2014).

When the company re-emerged from their hiatus in 2012 they constructed two types of performance events. They staged full-length plays, such as those they produce in legitimate theatre spaces. For example, their 2013 production of *Twelfth Night* was produced at the Actor's Theatre of Charlotte, and their ChicksBeer Series was also staged and is more akin to the original work presented by the company when it formed in 1998. The ChicksBeer Series work is highly popular in Charlotte and is a short combination of the plays performed at Noda Brewing Company 'similar to Reduced Shakespeare Company's pieces' in style and anarchic ribaldry:

> Our target audience for these are people who don't 'think' they would enjoy Shakespeare or those who haven't been exposed as much to his work. They come in, sit at table, drink good locally made Craft beer and enjoy food prepared by local Food Trucks. They sit back, drink, relax and we bring them some funny, bawdy, enjoyable pieces of the Bard's work – all performed by Chicks, of course. (Proctor 2014)

Working in an all-female context can present challenges for women, particularly when playing cross-gender roles. Imagine the nexus of considerations that is presented in a play like Chickspeare's *Twelfth Night* when a woman is cast as Viola and the character disguises herself as the male/boy role (Cesario) against women cast in legitimate (non-disguised) male roles, such as Orsino and Sebastian. Some single-sex companies, such as the all-male Propeller, create a theatrical device to frame the layered gendered performances or establish a training for the legitimate cross-dressing and foreground the disguise clearly such as in the Queen's Company model. Chickspeare's approach is more akin with that described by actors working on Lloyd's *Julius Caesar*:

> Approaching the characters is done mostly through motivation. What motivates the 'person' rather than merely this 'man' or 'woman'. Once the motivation/what drives the person is discovered, we place the character into the time period they are in and look at societal factors that may be placed on the character as a male or female in that particular period of time. For instance, the actors in roles for 'Twelfth Night' set in the United States during the Roaring 20's would be so different in their approach as opposed to its original setting. Women were becoming more vocal, had just gotten to vote, and were approaching life in a more non-traditional manner. The male and female characters had to take all this social context into consideration. Consequently, the exploration is all about the character rather than getting too obsessed with the thought 'I'm a woman playing a man'. It becomes 'I'm Orsino'. (Proctor 2014)

Although they admittedly have had their struggles as a company and often have to use their ingenuity and social media to gather attention, funding and audiences, Chickspeare has managed to move forward through tough challenges and establish their rightful place as a female-focused Shakespeare company. 'In a season when two all-male Shakespeare productions are running on Broadway, we have a counter-argument here in Charlotte that suggests all-female makes just as much sense' (*Creative Loafing Charlotte* 2013).

Though recasting Shakespeare's male roles with women makes 'sense', all-male companies enjoy a more legitimised and stable position in the theatre than that of the all-female companies profiled in this chapter. All-male Shakespeare companies can claim a historical focus and offer recreations as a result of their single-sex casting and Elizabethan theatrical practice. In contrast, all-female companies seem to struggle to claim such legitimacy despite having a rich history and practice. They are not trying to rewrite themselves into history but to shed light on a female-driven cross-gender tradition that existed, was successful and somehow lost over time.

These women-centred companies struggle to keep afloat in the patriarchal sea and therefore their work is unanimously moored in a feminist activism that aims to make their historical practice visible whilst providing a platform for women and girls to explore their performance of Shakespeare's male and female roles. They have made distinct contributions in the development and proliferation of performance practices to embody and play with gender and have created new avenues for reconsidering gender in the theatrical as well as social sphere.

8
Creative Casting

In the last two chapters we focused our discussion on contemporary single-sex companies and productions. In this chapter we will shift our focus to a discussion of selective, or what is at times referred to, creative casting choices. When we discuss selective or creative casting, we generally mean alternative non-traditional uses of casting that can take on a variety of forms and generate interesting effects on Shakespeare's plays for audiences.

Unlike using a single-sex model, mirroring Shakespeare's own theatrical practice, selectively or creatively casting a role or roles in a Shakespeare production, can produce new readings and freshen the plays. However, castings of this kind can be extraordinarily varied and many artists have a range of approaches and intentions for creatively casting cross-gender, but as a result there can be tensions that arise from such decisions including textual and performance considerations that have to be addressed.

Elizabeth Klett (2009) explains that there are several different approaches to cross-gender casting single-sex productions such as that of the Queen's Company or Hall's Propeller. For example, using selective casting (casting an actor against the gender of the character) and regendering (when a character is changed in the story to a different gender to match the casting). It is important for us to consider that these two approaches are distinct as they are often confused in discussions of practice and directorial concepts.

Companies in England tend to either employ single-sex casting (particularly with all-male companies and productions) or use selective casting to feature reputable actors in key roles. In addition to Fiona Shaw's undertaking of Richard II at the National and Kathryn Hunter's turn at

101

Lear, as discussed earlier, Vanessa Redgrave played Prospero in the 2000 SGT production directed by Lenka Udovicki. Although the production featured Redgrave in the title role, her character remained male, in the programme description. Interestingly, Redgrave's approach to the gender of the character wasn't decided when the casting was announced. Mark Rylance was the artistic director at the time and stated that the casting wasn't wholly a move to redress the gender imbalance at the Globe but rather he was interested in casting Redgrave as Prospero because it was:

> a part which her father played for the Royal Shakespeare Company five decades ago. Redgrave's personal humanitarian experience of aiding refugees from war-torn countries, he said, will make her that much more sympathetic to the role. (*Playbill* 18 January 2000)

Many critics agreed that Redgrave was an inspired choice, 'the casting of an actress who, on paper at least, is a tremendous prospect for the role' and that, in terms of embodying a masculine character, 'with her considerable frame and build, can easily suggest a mannish demeanor' (*Variety* 12 June 2000). Redgrave seemed destined to play the role.

Once the production choice to keep Prospero as male but not play the role as overtly masculine was announced, reviewers indicated that the concept created a conflicting message, polarising the critics. For some, like Nicholas De Jongh, Redgrave's performance highlighted the maternal connection to Miranda. 'Prospero is thoroughly Redgraved, transformed into a sweet eccentric who adores his daughter' (*The Evening Standard* 30 May 2000), and the actor's husky tone served to evoke a masculine presence. For others the effect was displaced, misguided and disruptive and, like Shaw's Richard II and Hunter's Lear, fell in the androgynous zone leaving the critics divided and questioning if selective casting improved or added positively to the performance of Shakespeare.

There was a sense from the critics that the casting of Redgrave disrupted the play and the effect of her 'feminine' sensibility conflated with her female 'masculine' credibility resulted in a confused performance.

> Prospero's appearance continued the impression that this production would de-emphasize illusory effects. Redgrave's exiled Duke had obtained a few wrinkles and stains over the years. Querulous, scattered, and not a little cranky, this Prospero curiously resembled, in voice, mannerisms, and costume, Tom Baker's beloved portrayal

of 'Dr. Who.' Such a Prospero was gratifyingly unconventional, although at times more low-key than one would wish from an actor usually so powerful. Redgrave's voice, low pitched, clear and flexible, nevertheless lacked the ringing command often inherent in the lines. Her Prospero's affection for Miranda was much more apparent than the character's anger over the past and his sinister anticipation of revenge to come. Redgrave chose an androgynous interpretation of the role that unfortunately robbed the character of the vengeful macho posturing that helps make his later reconciliations poignant. (McDermott 2000)

Like the sharp criticism aimed at Fiona Shaw's performance of the androgynous Richard II, Redgrave's performance was equally admonished for its lack of gender clarity. These issues may have risen due to an unclear approach for women when inhabiting male roles. In the case of Fiona Shaw's performance she made a conscious decision to perform an androgynous character, and this meant that the reviewers found the 'gender performance' vague and lacking something to attach their understanding to solidly. After all, how many androgynous people do they know? How many performances have they seen played in an androgynous way? Redgrave was attempting to play Prospero as male, but with her own understanding as a woman in the world and this was found equally confusing. Let's examine another, and arguably more successful version, of creatively casting a woman in the role of Prospero.

Demetra Pittman was cast as Prospero in the Oregon Shakespeare Festival's 2001 production of *The Tempest* directed by Penny Metropulos. In her introductory notes for the production, Metropulos asks, 'What would happen if we had no preconception of *The Tempest*?' Here she aims to direct the audience to watching the play afresh to 'see and hear this play for the first time'[1] and to do so through the lens of a non-traditional casting approach but without emphasising the regendering of the character. In this production, Prospero was regendered and the text had to be altered to address this alternative concept. In her description of the play, the director points to the regendering, guiding the audience through the narrative changes:

> When we first meet Prospero, she is obsessed with seeking revenge on her enemies ... She has landed on an island of magic, and the very qualities which destroyed her, politically, have turned into an enormous source of power for her. (Metropulos *Playbill* 2001: 8)

The use of the introduction and of female pronouns immediately sig-nals to the audience to abandon their 'preconceptions' and provides instruction on how they are to participate in experiencing the play 'for the first time'. She goes on to explain to the audience that 'Gender is not the issue of the production. Casting Prospero as a woman has only helped us explore the themes in a new light' (2001: 8). These themes include emphasising the familial bonds between Prospero and Miranda as well as Prospero and Antonio.

However, it is not just Prospero that was re-gendered in this pro-duction. In order to assist the text and the audience in following new themes inspired by the non-traditional casting, Prospero's usurping brother Antonio was transformed into Antonia and played by Linda Alper. This alteration meant that the production created new social dynamics between characters, shifting from father-daughter to 'mother-daughter, sister-sister and a woman acting with maternal rather than paternal passion' (*Salem Statesman's Journal* 2001), and introduced themes of forgiveness rather than that of revenge:

> Prospero has gone deep inside herself, alone on her island, to search her soul. She has raised her daughter; now it is time to face the world. By bringing her wrongdoers to her; she sets the stage for her re-entry to society. She must let go of her reclusive state; of her absolute powers over her tiny duchy, and that's scary. But only by forgiving her ene-mies, by letting go of control, can she take her rightful place as ruler of Milan. (*Eugene Weekly* 1 March 2001)

Director Metropulos took inspiration from Redgrave's 2000 perfor-mance but approached the production with clarity of purpose and gen-der. In regendering the role, she was able to bring fresh readings to the play and her work to signal to the Oregon Shakespeare Festival (OSF) audiences that the regendering was intentional, helped make the pro-duction a success and paved the way for future creative castings with the company.

Cross-gender casting in practice

The Oregon Shakespeare Festival was founded in 1935 by Angus L. Bowmer and has a long history of non-traditional casting. For example, the company has been employing gender-blind casting practices as far back as 1935 when Beth Cummings (Stephano) and Maxine Gearhart

(Magnifico) were cast in traditionally male roles in a production of *The Merchant of Venice* in OSF's Elizabethan Theatre. Reputedly the 'oldest and largest professional non-profit' (OSF website 2014) theatre company in the US, the festival has historically led the industry in making risky and bold theatrical choices, particularly with casting. Nestled in the hills of Southern Oregon, the festival and its artists gained a reputation amongst locals for their 'experimental' and diverse casting choices in the early 60s. Pat Patton, long-time OSF production manager and director, described the negative community response to the company's non-traditional racial casting choices as unsettling, 'even a white Oregon native didn't always feel at home', and that OSF artists were frequently referred to as 'the Shakesqueers' (*The Oregonian* 20 February 2010). Despite initial disdain from the Ashland locals for such provocative casting choices, OSF soldiered forward and, in doing so, changed minds and hearts. Today, Ashland and most of Southern Oregon embrace the festival and support its artistic choices and social focus.

OSF's commitment to diversity and inclusiveness has evolved and deepened over the past few decades as several artistic directors retained and expanded the company's aims 'to bring in a greater diversity of performers' (2010) to the festival, developing strategies and practices to do so:

> Henry Woronicz, named artistic director in 1991, made the hiring of more minority actors one of his top three goals. The push for diversity gathered energy under Libby Appel, who took over in 1995.

This commitment to diversity representation on OSF stages was particularly signalled in the hiring of Bill Rauch as artistic director of the company in 2007. Rauch's background running the community-based Cornerstone Theatre Company and directing projects that reflect a diverse American experience made him an ideal candidate to test questions such as, '"How much progress can we make in creating a theater that, in its work and in its audience, reflects our country?"' (*The New York Times* 14 August 2009).

These are some tough questions to tackle, but Rauch has his Cornerstone Theatre Company (CTC) experience to draw upon. In an interview with Rob Kendt Rauch discussed the heated public debates regarding community representation in the plays CTC was presenting. Of particular note was 'the controversy over the representation of gay Muslims in *A Long Bridge Over Deep Waters*' (Kendt 2006) and how the company created a forum with local Muslims to facilitate a debate presenting all sides of the complex issue.

> There were people inside and outside Cornerstone who said, 'There are gay Muslims, and we want to represent them in our play. It's a non-issue.' People were even insulted that we had to spend any time talking to anybody about it. And then there were people who said, 'It's a non-issue – the majority of the community has said, "This is offensive, this is against our religion, we don't want it in our play." Why would Cornerstone even think about dragging a gay Muslim into the mix?' So you had these two completely contradictory worldviews, both of which were dismissive of the fact that the company would take the time to investigate both points of view. (2006)

Despite the community's neglect to recognise the poignancy and effort the company had made, Rauch found the experience of facilitating such an event with the community rewarding and aims to create opportunities in his approach and programming at OSF 'where I'm having those conversations' (2006).

Rauch's approach stems from a philosophical sense that theatre should be 'community based', reflective and responsive to, and at times against popular sentiment, locally and globally. He also argues that 'all art is political with some more or less obvious what the politics are, or what's being attempted' (Gross *TheatreTimes.org* May 2014). This philosophy is positively reinforcing OSF's efforts to not only stage a multifarious view of the American experience through the selection of cutting edge, often marginalised stories and new plays, such as those commissioned for the American Revolutions initiative, but also cut into representational models of excellence wherein a multicultural picture is reflected – even in the casting choices made with actors. In their approach to the staging of Shakespeare's plays, we see a number of exceptional casting choices that include variations of gender performances being played out before OSF audiences.

One prime example is the 2011 production of *Julius Caesar* directed by Amanda Dehnert and starring Vilma Silva in the role of Caesar. Like Metropulos' *The Tempest* in 2001, the casting was approached through a regendering of the role of Caesar and required textual revision and a firm signal to OSF audiences about the choice in casting. Vilma Silva was cast as Caesar in director Amanda Dehnert's production in order to 'shake up gender roles and comment on gender politics' (Guzik *Ashland Daily Tidings* 16 April 2011) as well as to shift the story from focus on a male-dominated politicised Rome to demonstrating 'that leadership is a human story, not just a male story' (2011).

The regendering of Caesar wasn't initially intentional but came about as a result of OSF's repertory casting process wherein actors in the company perform in several productions during the season. The director 'decided to cast the strongest actor for the role, without focusing on gender. Once she decided Silva should play Caesar, the role began to expand, offering a comment on women in leadership' (2011), and the process of changing the text to match Silva's female Caesar began. This caused a bit of confusion for the actors in the rehearsal room. 'During the first week of rehearsal for the Oregon Shakespeare Festival's production of "Julius Caesar", the actors kept accidentally referring to the Roman dictator as "She-sar"' (2011). However, it was quickly understood that this casting choice and adaptation of Shakespeare's *Julius Caesar* offered a story that was remarkably poignant and timely, as several notable women in leadership roles were being questioned, even assassinated, over their adoption of power and privilege in patriarchal societies:

> Just as the play's famously anachronistic clock brought the play into the present for the Elizabethans, Silva's Caesar resonates for us in the present because we've seen the assassinations of Benazir Bhutto and Indira Ghandi. (*Medford Mail Tribune* 28 March 2011)

The director also 'cast other women in roles typically played by men, including some of Caesar's conspirators' (Guzik 2011). Dehnert explains that she made this casting choice 'consciously' in an effort to 'ensure that this was a mixed gender story' (2011). The play also included a mixed race as well as mixed gender cast, and these choices helped 'to comment on gender roles and racial stereotypes .... Opening up both gender and race in this staging is simply meant to allow us to see it as universal' (2011).

As with Metropolos' *The Tempest*, the critics found the regendering, cross-casting and overall directorial vision favourable, even declaring that the actor's 'sex is irrelevant' (*Rosy's Theatre Reviews* 2011) and seemingly embraced the fresh modern perspective given to the classical piece:

> Ms Dehnert's nondoctrinaire approach to high-concept theatre is exemplified by the way she uses Ms. Silva. Her 'Julius Caesar' is not a tendentious study of Women in Power in which Shakespeare's verse is relegated to the status of background music, but a production

whose Caesar happens to be played by a woman. (Teachout *The Wall Street Journal* 26 August 2011)

Following *Julius Caesar*, Rauch took experimentation and gender casting to extremes when he staged *Medea/Macbeth/Cinderella* as part of the 2012 OSF season. Conceived in his mind when he was an undergraduate student at Harvard, and inspired by director Peter Sellers,[2] Rauch wanted to create a piece of theatre that combined the three 'great movements in populist drama' (Steffan *Portland Mercury* 19 April 2012). Working with dramatist Tracey Young to bring the production to life they laid 'the three texts side by side', finding 'significant overlap in shared themes: royal ambition, magic, transformation, parent/child relations and the roles of women in a male-dominated society' (Shirley *LAStageTimes.com* 2012). The experimental nature of the piece allowed for creativity in casting as well: 'the cast of the *Medea* part is entirely female, while the cast of the *Macbeth* part is entirely male' (2012).

In early 2014, I interviewed dramaturg Lydia Garcia, in her seventh season at the Oregon Shakespeare Festival, to gain an insider's perspective on the company's evolving diversity profile and commitment to equal gender representation on its stages.

TP: Have you noticed changes over the seven seasons you have been with the company in terms of gender representation on stage?

LG: One thing that Luis (Alfaro) is always saying is that here at OSF we cast all ways – always. So we're always playing with different casting models and sometimes gender choices, race, ethnicity choices are specific for a production because they are meant to evoke something for the audience in terms of the story in a new or insightful way. Or sometimes we are casting based on skill, based on interest, or which actor is best suited for a role.

Garcia points to a few examples from her seasons with the company wherein directors made unique casting choices. These examples included Bill Rauch's production of *Hamlet* in 2010 in which he cast two women as Rosencrantz and Guildenstern, and Garcia also cites the 2011 production of *Julius Caesar*, 'that was probably, at that point, the boldest choice up until then'.

Garcia has been interested in the topic of cross-gender casting and has researched the company's history to reflect on such diversity in casting approaches. She investigated 'the number of times women had been cast in traditionally male roles' and from her records concludes:

> LG: It seemed that, for the most part, the male roles that were being cast with women were the minor smaller roles, so for example, Dee Maske as Adam in *As You Like It*, or certainly the comedies like Peter Quince, Starveling (*A Midsummer Night's Dream*) but it's not until you get to 2001 and you have a female Prospero, or you get to 2011 and you see a female Julius Caesar.

She also notes some interesting ancillary performances such as Kimberly Scott's portrayal of Charles the Wrestler in *As You Like It*. Scott played the role as a man but 'just happens to be a female performer'. Later in our interview Garcia explains her interest in this particular performance:

> LG: I found it so fascinating talking to audience members and just asking 'do you remember who played Charles the Wrestler?' and for the most part nobody figured out that it was Kimberly Scott – which was tremendous and, of course, you know that the following season, just last year, the same actor was again playing with gender representations in *The Liquid Plain*, which was a new play by Naomi Wallace where we are first introduced to her as a man who then is revealed to be a woman living as a man.

Garcia finds such castings fascinating and an important aspect to the repertory model. For the audience it must be a unique experience watching an actor shift from a Shakespeare comedy to a new play using gender performance practice modes as a running commentary. This kind of experience is unique, and it seems the company is moving into a period, 'where questions of gender presentation are at the forefront' of an ongoing community dialogue.

During her research investigation Garcia also found it interesting to see how the company played with gender historically and why and when they 'choose to change the gender of a character from male to female, and when we the simply put a female body in to play a man'.

As a resident dramaturg at OSF, one of her tasks involves working closely with directors and aiding them as they make integral decisions in casting or applying a unique director's concept that may require alterations in the text. Sometimes Garcia is privy to unique casting choices before the start of the rehearsal and the preparatory process, but other times such decisions were not shared in advance and that necessitates her sitting down with the director to discuss the effect that the casting choices make on the text. For example, when a director has cast a woman in a role that is traditionally male, she usually has to pose some pointed questions: 'Are you interested in changing the gender? In changing the pronouns? Are you interested in simply leaving the text as is? And just having an assistant or woman uttering those lines. Are you interested in having her put on facial hair and playing a man and what does that mean?' Some directors have already thought this through and can easily offer answers and solutions, whereas others have not considered the impact of the casting choices on the production.

Garcia worked closely with Bill Rauch on *Measure for Measure* in 2011 providing dramaturgical support and advice during the casting and text work process. In our interview she described the process and how some of the cross-gender choices came to fruition and affected the story being told:

> **LG:** He (Bill Rauch) was very interested in exploring a socially, cul-
> turally, gender-conscious way of casting the show to get at what
> he thought were central issues of that play. So when he thought
> about casting Escalus with a woman and switching the gender
> of Escalus from a man to a woman, we talked a little about how
> that would effect the power dynamics between the Duke, between
> Escalus and Angelo ... What happens if Angelo is a young Latino
> man? Okay, what happens if Isabella is a young Latino woman?
> We talked about Mistress Overdone, for example, because there
> was a long-time actor in the company who was interested in this
> character of Mistress Overdone. What if he were to portray her as
> a man who chooses to live his life as a woman?
>
> And so that became a whole different layer of complexity for
> us to explore. We recognized in so many ways that gender pres-
> entation, gender expression, is a social structure; is a social con-
> struct of course, and what happens if we see the consequences of
> Mistress Overdone being arrested, and we see her being processed
> in the police station, and she is systematically stripped of her wig
> and her clothes and everything that presents who she is in the
> world. Down to her body that just happens to be a male body,
> but that's not how she sees herself. Bill was very interested in talk-
> ing through all of those nuances and testing to see how I would
> respond, because I am not only an artist in the process but an
> audience member. And a woman in the world, and a woman of
> color in the world, so you know, how I respond to things is often
> very unvarnished. It was a really fulsome conversation.

At OSF sometimes in a season the company has over 100 actors working in repertory and this necessitates non-traditional casting choices, particularly in the works of Shakespeare, as there are so few female roles for the women to play. Often, women are cast as male characters, or characters are regendered in these productions to address the gender disparity, but the roles that are cross-cast or adapted tend to be ancillary ones.

Similar practices are at play in other large regional and national theatre companies such as at the RSC in England. In 2013, I met actor Debbie Korley during a workshop with the company and we spoke briefly about her experience working in the repertory company at the RSC. We discussed the fact that she had to sometimes play small male roles, when she was also portraying large female roles such as Cordelia in *King Lear*. At the time of our conversation I had wondered how actors that are given these roles might reconcile the casting in their approach. Seizing the opportunity to discuss this thought, I posed the question to Garcia:

TP: Do these actors feel they are just 'paying their dues' when they get cross-cast in large productions?

LG: That's a good question. I think, for the most part, the Shakespeare productions that have happened while I have been here, where I have seen gender swaps, like in a major character [such as] in *As You Like It* having the character of Jacques played by a woman, it made the relationship between Duke Sr. and Orsino … it gave it some nuances that were very lovely. And certainly in terms of us following Jacques' journey, and where 'she' is at the end of that play, and Duke Sr. is about to leave this world and be reunited with his kingdom, and his daughter and the rest of his family, and Jacques feels left out of that. So it gave us a different take on this character that so often is played as being surly, and always in opposition to whatever the world is heading.

We also discussed the question of audiences' reaction to the adaptations, regendering and cross-casting. Garcia painted a very positive picture explaining that 'for the most part audiences take it in stride'.

LG: They take their cues from us. If we announce that Vilma Silva will be playing Julius Caesar next year and inhabit the 'of course she will be playing Julius Caesar cause she's the incredible Vilma Silva and she will be tremendous in that role', that might get ahead of the push back of 'why in the world are you having a woman playing the role of Julius Caesar? Is it a bit of stunt casting? What are we trying to say about women in leadership? What are we trying to say about the relationship between Julius Caesar and Mark Anthony, and Brutus?' And certainly we can't discount that because any time we put a body on stage that body has meaning, and if that body happens to be female, if that body happens to be a body of color, we ascribe meaning to it.

She also discussed the effect of cross-casting and regendering Shakespeare through a personal perspective, explaining that when she saw Silva as Julius Caesar it was as though it 'was the first time' she saw the play. The experience made her aware of 'how much is projected onto Caesar by other people' and that 'seeing a female body and hearing how the others were talking about Caesar, and the … plotting and the rancor of "how dare Caesar wield power over us" by having it be a woman' gave her the experience of 'hearing it very differently'. The contemporary context was highlighted and current parallels were easily drawn:

> LG: In 2011 Benazir Bhutto had been assassinated not too long before we chose that play, and she was front and center in my mind as we were getting ready for that production.

OSF continues to experiment with a variety of non-traditional casting practices aiming to step away from stereotypical assumptions of sex and gender, whilst marking their stages more inclusive and reflective of the multicultural world in which their audiences inhabit. Expanding beyond just creatively casting a few roles in a production, in 2014 the company staged their first all-female Shakespeare play *Two Gentlemen of Verona* directed by Sarah Rasmussen. Also referred to as 'No Gents', Rasmussen called the production 'a playful parallel' to Shakespeare's all-male company and explained that she wanted to direct Shakespeare that would give talented female actors to play beyond the limited 'ingenues and nursemaids' (Rasmussen as quoted in Lawton's article for *Theatre Communications Group* 2014).

Staged in the 1,200-seat Globe-inspired Allen Elizabethan Theatre the production centred on the 'Gentlemen' of Verona, exploring questions of what it meant to be a 'man' in Shakespeare's Verona and, in part, in the Elizabethan era. In the hands of an all-female cast the play illuminated 'questions of gender and forgiveness' and Rasmussen likened the experience to 'listening to a new band cover and old song – we are simultaneously honoring the lyrics and hearing them in a whole new way' (2014).

The production was, as Bunnell (*The Lone Penman* 5 August 2014) describes in his review, the 'season's most conservative Shakespeare ... except that it's presented by an all-female cast' and did little to disguise the women's bodies beneath the Elizabethan-inspired costumes: 'only one secondary character sports a fake goatee, and most of the women wear their natural hair, cut short or elaborately pinned' (Bachrach *Oregon ArtsWatch* 22 August 2014). It was also obvious that their physicality and voicework was not trained for cross-gender performance in the same way as that of the all-female companies featured in the last chapter:

> There are no codpieces, no exaggerated leg-splaying. Only once is sudden shrillness of voice used for comic effect, and even then, it is not a jab at the woman hidden in the guise of 'Proteus,' but the boy still lurking beneath the man that Proteus is trying so hard to become.

The 'opportunity to hear' Shakespeare's verse and prose 'through the bodies of extraordinary artists who otherwise would not have the chance' (Clark as quoted in Lawton's article for *Theatre Communications Group* 2014) to perform in such roles was part of the unique concept explored in the production and highlighted the challenges of masculine gender performativity on stage and within the *Two Gentlemen of Verona* narrative. In her review of the production Bachrach (2014) explains:

> But while Gomez and Clark don't seek to embody any kind of stereotypical maleness, watching Valentine and Proteus fumble to flirt, dance, and fit in at court through female bodies is a constant and striking reminder that the title of 'gentleman' to which they aspire is no more (or less) natural to a pair of men than it is to the pair of women playing them. Their comic failures are in pursuit of an impossible ideal: They can no more become the 'perfect gentleman' their fathers long for than Gomez and Clark can.

This failure of masculinity in the performance of gender roles serves the narrative well and evokes a deeper meaning when played out before an audience. One of the most challenging considerations when staging *Two Gentlemen of Verona* for a contemporary audience is negotiating the final act when Proteus attempts to rape Sylvia, his best friend Valentine's girlfriend, and then repents his actions and is forgiven by all quite suddenly. In the OSF production the all-female cast brings a deeper sense of shame and embarrassment to this act, and the effect is profound and evokes a sense of truth:

> For the first time, I found Proteus's sudden horror at what he has become to be convincing. This is due in large part to Clark's tremendous performance, which leads us to the obvious dissonance between Proteus and his ideal self in the text. His increasing panic about this disconnect explodes naturally, and when it ebbs, the regret that remains feels clear-eyed and truthful. (Bachrach 2014)

The 'No Gents' all-female production was the first of its kind at OSF and hopefully not the last. Despite concerns that an all-female production at OSF might not 'be good', 'hold' or 'sell tickets' (Lawton 2014), Rasmussen's direction enlivened the comedy and highlighted the gender conflicts within the story with a great deal of success. Audiences bought tickets, the cast received critical praise and K.T. Vogt was awarded the Falstaff Award for best supporting performance (2014) as the comical servant Launce. The production demonstrated that by casting differently sexed actors in cross-gender roles, new meanings and fresh perspectives from the text can transpire to help contemporary audiences accept some sticky areas in Shakespeare's texts, such as that of the attempted rape of Sylvia in *Two Gentlemen of Verona*. Like OSF, the Judith Shakespeare Company also uses regendering and selective casting of differently sexed actors to play roles in Shakespeare's plays and, in 2010, tastefully tackled these issues in their production of *Two Gentlemen of Verona*.

Regendering and cross-casting Shakespeare's characters can elicit contemporised readings of his plays, but it is interesting to note that these practices tend to be employed more prevalently in the USA than in the UK. For example, although regendering as a practice may be occurring in experimental and fringe productions in the UK, it is interesting to note that most major regional theatres are creatively cross-casting selected roles rather than 'rewriting' Shakespeare, and this practice is still rare at high-profile theatres.

However, there are a handful of companies willing to take such imaginative casting leaps such as in the approach taken by the Royal Exchange Theatre in Manchester, England, with the casting of Maxine Peake as Hamlet in Sarah Frankcom's 2014 production. Rather than regendering *Hamlet*, in the preproduction press and interviews, the theatre called it a 'radical re-imaging of *Hamlet*' (the Royal Exchange Theatre website 2014) and it was unclear how casting a woman in the role, given the rich history of women that have played Hamlet historically, made it a 'radical' staging.

Perhaps the creative casting choice was a radical move forward for the northern England company, but even this argument falls short when we consider that the Royal Exchange Theatre was the only regional theatre to report to British Equity that it offered 'increased opportunities for women' and had 'employed more actresses than actors in 2009/10' (Trueman *The Independent* 17 November 2012).

Susannah Clapp of *The Observer* (20 September 2014) notes that the increase of women's visibility and casting in male roles in productions at companies like The Royal Exchange Theatre and the Donmar have possibly to do with the increased number of female directors and management at these theatres stating that:

> Frankcom is in effect creating England's first mainstream feminist theatre. She has done so not only by cross-casting but by her choice of plays, among them *The Last Days of Troy* and *Orlando*.

In an interview, Maxine Peake discussed the initial motivations behind the casting of *Hamlet* (2014), citing her close connection to the theatre and its leader Sarah Frankcom:

> Sarah and I have looked for a project that would stretch and excite us and Hamlet just seemed the next natural step to challenge us both in so many ways. I am so excited how gender swapping can affect and throw up new ways of looking at this theatrical masterpiece. (Bourke *Creativetourist.com* 2014)

This statement is echoed in the discussions of many artists working to reconsider Shakespeare through creatively casting and regendering characters. Indeed, new insights can be discovered in these productions, but such casting approaches can also empower actors and make larger contributions to the industry. Maxine Peake discusses the unequal treatment in cross-gender performance between male and female actors:

> When there are all-male companies doing Shakespeare, no one minds and no one should bat an eye if a woman plays Hamlet or Henry V … We're actors doing a part and, on stage now in 2014, it's about time there was a freedom to do that. When else are female actors going to get an opportunity to do those great speeches? So far, men have had all the fun! (2014)

The creative casting of *Hamlet* (2014) extended beyond the casting of Peake in the role of Hamlet. Frankcom's reimagined production included 'a Player Queen (the powerful and mellifluous Claire Benedict), female gravediggers (Michelle Butterly is a jaunty Scouser) and a knowing biker of a Rosencrantz (Jodie McNee)'. Frankcom also regendered Ophelia's father Polonius, changing him to 'Polonia' played by Gillian Bevan 'as a fusspot, continually tweaking her dark suit into place and accompanying her orotund phrases with redundant flourishes of her hands' (Clapp *The Observer* 20 September 2014).

Similar to OSF's *Two Gentlemen of Verona* (2014), the presence of female actors in Shakespeare's male roles amplified the issues of gender performativity within the play's narrative. Lawson of the *New Statesman* (26 September 2014) explains that the cross-gendering 'brings some interpretive gains' and the unique casting demonstrates that 'part of Hamlet's problem is a struggle with society's definitions of masculinity'. Rosencrantz and Guildenstern hint at Hamlet's homosexuality, and the play conveys his 'unease at female sexuality' which many actors have used interpretively to play Hamlet as feminised or sexually ambiguous. Peake's portrayal of Hamlet was both delicate and fierce, and it is this balance between the feminine actor and the masculine role that allowed her performance to 'amplify' Hamlet's sexual ambiguity and social gender failure as expressed in the text. Clapp (2014) describes Peake as 'a stripling prince, almost pre-sexual, who glides, without swagger and without girlishness' but this is where most comparisons between the two productions end.

Peake's Hamlet was initially approached with an attempt at embodying the male role through physical and psychological choices. She cut her hair short, spoke in deeper tones than her normal speaking voice (Lawson 2014), bound her breasts and was 'a damn good fencer' (Clapp 2014). The production was in modern dress but this may have proved distracting; Cavendish (*The Telegraph* 17 September 2014) noted that 'the blue jacket and trousers' she wore evoked 'a melancholy pierrot' and that she looked 'sensational, the sort of pale-faced stunner Vivienne Westwood would rush to wrap in Tartan'. From the interviews and reviews, it doesn't seem that 'sexual ambiguity' was the aim in Peake's portrayal but more a residual effect of the star's presence in the role.

The biggest criticism of the production was not the selective casting of Peake in the title role, but of the approach to casting and regendering of the ancillary characters. Cavendish (2014) questions the choices presented:

But if Hamlet remains, technically, male in this reading – why make these added distinctions? Kissing Rosencrantz and Ophelia on the lips? Yes, OK, so? Wouldn't it be more radical, and interesting, for the rest of the company to be male? Or for the central switch to look more anomalous?

Perhaps, but isn't it equally anomalous for companies to play with gender casting and put women in a variety of non-traditional roles and in unexpected ways such as regendering as well as selective casting? I believe so and have seen such variations at play before audiences in the work of New York's Judith Shakespeare Company.

The Judith Shakespeare Company

The Judith Shakespeare Company was founded by Joanne Zipay in an effort to create more opportunities for classically trained women to perform in professional productions in New York City. Zipay had studied Shakespeare at the University of San Diego's Old Globe Theatre. Frustrated with the lack and depth of roles offered to women when 'traditional' gender casting was applied to productions, Zipay decided to launch her own company and force an emphasis on promoting women in the classical tradition.

> Joanne has always cast women in interesting ways, including using women to play all the kings in *The History Cycle* – a series of eight plays that the company produced from 2002–2004 – about 100 years of war and five different English kings. It's not that the role is now a woman; it's that the actor playing the role is a woman. (Hack *The Brooklyn Rail* 2010)

The company has endured since 1995 despite some shifts in its management, along with a financially imposed hiatus when they were seeking funding. Initially the company was conceived of as one that would expand opportunities for women . This aim developed into a variety of casting styles as Zipay and her team began to widen their reach as a company. Over time, she developed an interest in 'open casting' as an approach and her company began to, from time to time, institute a gender-blind colour-blind focus whilst still keeping women at the centre of their work.

In 2010, the company produced a unique gender-reversed *Two Gentlemen of Verona* that included men playing the female roles alongside the women playing the leading male ones. For the company this was a clear 'move forward' and for Zipay artistically the casting exercise engendered an adventurous freshness in direction, 'taking on romantic comedy and reverse gender'. I conducted a personal interview with Zipay in early 2014 and we discussed the production and the company's casting approach.

> **TP:** Tell me a little bit more about that production because that is a very unique way of approaching women's representation in Shakespeare but putting gender on its head.

> **JZ:** I had been thinking about Two Gents for a long time because we had done the entire history cycle. We had been doing really heavy stuff for awhile. It was the lightest show I could possibly think of in contrast to all the very heavy stuff. And as I worked preparing for that, and every time I read the script, I kept thinking 'how am I going to reverse gender this?' because the things that they say are so male and the women say things that are so female. It's beautifully written for the words to come out of the mouths of, I think, very young teenage men and women. I kept reading it thinking 'I don't know if I can make this work', but that actually became the challenge and fun of it.

Two Gentlemen of Verona wasn't the first cross-gender production the company had staged that included men; the company 'had done a number of cross-gender things by then' starting with *Julius Caesar* in 1999 and 2000, but it was the first time employed in romantic comedy.

> **JZ:** I knew for a long time that I wanted to do something that I was calling 'Contemporary Commedia dell'arte'. I wanted to do something that had Commedia in the piece and not have it be leather masks and all that. So we worked to find a physical style to embrace (the genre) and then I framed the piece with the idea that it was a group of actors coming out to put on their costumes for the play. We had this whole opening number with the dog and everything, and started off with a woman holding up a man's costume thinking to herself 'how fun it would be'. And then it became sort of a game, and one of the guys sort of challenged everybody by starting to put on a woman's costume, and then the other guy was actually dressed by the women, and then the other man, he sort of did it on a dare because the other men were doing it.

She went on to explain that in the production there were three men playing the 'female roles' and that the Commedia device alongside the cross-gender performance framing 'game' aided the audiences' understanding of the layers of performativity the actors were playing with in the piece.

At the start, the actors were in their original clothes 'but then the men had corsets and skirts over that'. During the opening sequence, the female actors also dressed in the 'manly costumes', and layered on and played with, the gender signifiers in a playful and intriguing pre-show context aimed at the audience.

> JZ: You saw it all happening on two levels; you were in on the joke right from the very beginning. Actors came and went on the sidelines of the piece, watching, observing. They came out to see how the guy was going to pull off Silvia, and they changed the set ... so it had a Commedia feel to it. It was a Commedia world, which also allowed for us to be somewhat self-conscious with the gender reverse.

Zipay's use of the Commedia device at the start of the play aided the audience in reading and accepting the gender play on stage during the production. The constructed genders were playfully explored and allowed layers of meaning and inhabitation to add to the meta-theatricality of the performances.

> JZ: What actually resulted from it, which was astounding, was that it was very very believable. Which you wouldn't think from something that sounds so theatrical, but because it was framed the way it was the audience didn't have to say 'oh how good is this person doing playing a man or how good is this person doing playing a woman?' We worked to find the essence of the characters and who they were as people. And we also worked very hard on the physical behavior of the characters. We tried to find truthful behavior that wasn't campy. That wasn't mocking of the people that they were playing ... they had to find who their character was at first from the inside, and then find the truth of the characters through that mask of gender.

> TP: I can see how cross-casting would draw out the humour in the play, but how did you maneuver through the implied rape of Sylvia in Act Five?

> JZ: It was a little tricky. Our Sylvia was actually a lovely lovely actor and really found the sweetness, vulnerability, and the passion in

Sylvia and walked that fine line. It was really beautiful what he did without it being campy at all. It was pretty magnificent. But when it came to staging that scene we still had the challenge of it. I mean obviously he's a man with upper body strength, and how do we have this woman playing a man really come off as physically threatening? My fight choreographer is very very good, Dan O'Driscoll, and we used a ladder for many things in the play ... and so in the forest it was the tree that Valentine sits in ... and we used that tree for Proteus to back Sylvia up against so that she could be pushing backwards, and then Proteus pushing forward so that Proteus' upper body strength was more apparent than Sylvia's, and it worked.

Using the ladder to entrap Sylvia the female actor playing Proteus was able to corner the actor, pressing him up against the ladder to gain leverage and power over his prey. The effect worked and many audience members found the moment equally as disturbing as when the roles are normatively cast according to the gender of the actors. Zipay handled this moment through the play-within-the play device, offering the effect that the female 'Commedia' actor had taken her assumed masculine role and lust for power too far, and Valentine's disruption of the attempted rape was the sobering moment wherein the actor playing Proteus and, as detailed in the text, the character in the play realise their transgression. The framing concept served to make the moment more believable for a contemporary audience and, in a sense, easier to justify Proteus' immediate remorse and Valentine's sudden forgiveness of this vile act aimed at Sylvia.

> TP: In regard to your gender-blind casting policies, can you just talk to me a little bit about how you go about casting actors in roles?

> JZ: It varies from production to production. We've done a lot of gender-blind casting, which took me a long time to come around to because I don't think that you can toss away gender in a Shakespeare play. I think you've got to deal with it because it is an essential part of how the dramatic action is driven forward. Gender has a lot to do with the choices people make depending on whether they are men or women.

When approaching *The History Cycle*, a three-year project, she decided to cast all eight plays gender-blind for maximum fluidity and opportunity. Over time she was thrilled to verify her idea that 'no matter what happens you can use the best actor for the role'. Generally, when casting, she relies upon a consistent group of actors that she knows well and has worked with in past productions but also opens her calls to the wider theatre community whenever possible. As a result of her open-casting policy, she is sometimes surprised at what the actors bring to the auditions and this challenges her own preconceptions about a role or actor.

When casting Cymbeline she had wanted to cast it 'fairly straight'.

> JZ: I put the call out to my company to see who was available. I got responses from some guys, but I didn't really have ... Posthumus. I didn't have an Iachimo. I didn't have a Cloten among the men who were available, and then I looked at the women I had available and I said Jane's got to do Iachimo, and Natasha could do Posthumus, and Brady could do Cloten.

The result was that she ended up with a man playing Cymbeline, and the rest of the roles were played by women. This casting wasn't preconceived but happened as a result of her process of casting the best actors for the roles regardless of their normative gender. At times Zipay has preconceived ideas of how she wants to cast a show but has to revise her casting considerations when she discovers in the audition process that the 'best' actor for a role isn't what she might have originally wanted.

> JZ: For *Richard III* I read men for Margaret because I really wanted to have a male Margaret, and read women for Clarence ... The best actor for Clarence turned out to be a man and the best actor for Margaret turned out to be a woman. So that's who I cast.

During the company's staging of *The History Cycle*, she worked alongside another director but they shared many of the same actors. Zipay found it interesting that they cast quite differently from one another, and because there were a large number of roles to fill requiring actors to play multiple parts, sometimes in the same production, actors were cast in a variety of genders and configurations:

> We had men playing women, men playing men, Women playing women, women playing men, same sex couples, we had reverse gender couples, we had straight couples ... it was very fluid.

Achieving gender fluidity on our stages can be a complex endeavour for many regional theatres particularly if they produce Shakespeare plays in repertory. If they use traditional normative gender casting of roles, this can result in very few opportunities being offered to women and an extreme gender imbalance occurs.

Schilt and Westbrook explain that when we employ normative gender processes and 'expectations for men and women', onstage and off, we 'maintain gender inequality, as strictures of masculinity push men to "do dominance" and strictures of femininity push women to "do submission"' (2009: 443). These acts reinforce patriarchal power and privilege and as OSF actor Sofia Jean Gomez (2014) argues, 'male voices and a very old – yet highly prevalent – vision of "what women are to be"' is upheld when we cast in the 'old school' normatively gendered manner.

All of the companies featured in this chapter are theatre renegades, striving to break new ground by using creative casting approaches to address issues of inequality on their stages and, by extension, probing us to reconsider gender altogether. They are using a variety of creative casting approaches to readdress the gender balance in productions of Shakespeare and are 'on the path to not only continuing the conversation but enlightening, engaging, and provoking communities to expand and hopefully, change the view of Gender in theatre' (Gomez as quoted in Lawton's article for *Theatre Communications Group* 2014).

9
Queer Shakespeare

'No doubt Shakespeare was gay. His predilection was evident from his works. An unmistakenly feminine portrait of his patron Henry Wriothesley adds evidence that early sonnets to "fair youth" were probably meant for males' (Ian McKellen *Advocate* 5 January 2012). Many Queer scholars, artists and enthusiasts argue that Shakespeare is inherently Queer. His sexuality has been a recurrent area of speculation and part of a debate that we may never resolve. Many Shakespeare pro-gay advocates, such as Ian McKellen, are convinced that he was a gay man living in a heteronormative and homophobic society which caused him to be closeted in his personal life, but 'out' or rather 'hinted' at being a practising homosexual in his public plays and sonnets. These advocates point to particular works as demonstrating homosexual proclivities and alliances:

> *The Merchant of Venice*, centering on how the world treats gays as well as Jews, has a love triangle between an older man, younger man and a woman. And complexity in his comedies with cross-dressing and disguises is immense. Shakespeare obviously enjoyed sex with men as well as women. (McKellen 2012)

What we know from surviving records is that he was married to Anne Hathaway, fathered several children, and wrote arguably passionate sonnets dedicated to a mysterious 'Mr W. H', and his epic poem *Venus and Adonis* was written for the Henry Wriothesly, Earl of Southampton. Although his relationship with Wriothesly is predominately seen as an economic one (the Earl was his patron) the nature of the male-to-male intimacy he expresses in his poems and plays is at the heart of the great 'was Shakespeare homosexual?' question.

In Elizabethan England homo-social relationships between men were strikingly different from today, as were expectations of 'manliness' and masculinity. Men wore clothing that we might consider 'effeminate' today, including lace, satin, ruffs, stockings and earrings. Male friendships also were very different from those now as they included writing poetry and dedicating works to one another. When playing the role of Valentine in *Two Gentlemen of Verona* (2004) at the RSC, Alex Avery purports in his archived notes on the production that the friendship between Valentine and Proteus was differently expressed than that of friendships today:

> I think it's at a time when the love between two men is a greater love for some reason. There seems to be a sense from what I've read that the function of a male/female relationship is purely for the family and to procreate, to have a family. But a love between two men is something that you choose. You have arranged marriages, and I suppose what I'm saying is that a friendship between two men is created by the desires and wills of those two men, whereas a relationship between a man and a girl is actually probably constructed completely peripheral to whatever the feelings of the said boy and girl are. (RSC Learning document 2005: 11)

This was an aspect of the cultural ideology of Elizabethan gentlemanly 'love' at play, within the play that Shakespeare penned. Our reading of this manly devotion is that it is quite queer, but that has more to do with our cultural ideals and expectations of men than what Shakespeare and his peers were experiencing. Historically we do not know if Shakespeare's 'queerness', found throughout his plays, was intentional or, more likely, a modern Queer reading of his plays.

This reading is understandable given the close connectivity between what Lublin (2012) calls Shakespeare's 'transvestite theatre' and contemporary Queer discourse. In the introduction to *Cast Out: Queer Lives in Theatre* (2006), Robin Bernstein argues that, 'If queerness is inherently theatrical and theatre is inherently queer, then theatre and queerness always have and always will intertwine' (2006: 9). If we review Shakespeare's plays and theatrical practice with a Queer lens and accept that as the works are theatrical they are inherently queer, then the plays' content, subjects and characters reveal hallmarks of 'queerness' through the Queer lens. We apply Queer discourses to his works and participate in the 'queering' of Shakespeare, not only through our reading of his plays but through layers of practice including cross-gender performances and the staging of queer representations and narratives.

In our Queering of Shakespeare, we can reread his plays and stage them in non-traditional ways to highlight contemporary issues and experiences of queer 'otherness'. For example, the emphasis on cross-dressing and disguise in Shakespeare's plays has parallels to contemporary queer narratives – that of hiding a true identity from the wider world – known as being 'closeted'. Many of Shakespeare's characters 'disguise' themselves in his plays and often through the use of a cross-gender persona, in order to gain access or privilege in a world that suppresses their true nature. Not only is this expressed in the plays through the plot, but when such actions are performed by actors on the stage, the multiple layers of disguise and gender performance create profound social and theatrical meanings. Shakespeare was aware of the power of such a device and, we may argue, uses 'gender performativity' as a theatrical dialogue between actors and audience, questioning gender norms and also exploring homoerotic playing in a safe theatrical space. This theatrical practice can be Queerly read as revealing the impulses and desires of a playwright living in a repressive homophobic culture, but finding freedom in expressing his true nature through the workings of theatre.

Articulations, of self-censorship in an exterior world and gender expressivity in an interior safe space, mirrors Queer theatrical practice today. Lesbian, gay, bisexual, transgendered and queer (LGBTQ) people historically have faced discrimination and violence in unaccepting societies, and therefore many LGBTQ people have remained hidden or 'closeted' globally. Examples of living queer secret lives are found in plays and films such as *Boys Don't Cry*, *Angels in America*, *The Crying Game* and *Normal*. All of these works present characters, autobiographical and fictional, that have to hide their true gender and sexual identities as a result of cultural expectations and prejudice. In many of these stories, once the characters reveal their queer identities, bodies or sexualities they are met with disgust, abhorrence and even physical violence. In the case of Brandon Teena in *Boys Don't Cry*, the FTM (female to male) transgendered youth was raped and murdered by his peers once they discovered he was born biologically female. The repercussions of such gender and sexual transgressions in heteronormative society serve as a chilling yet common plot point in these pieces. These works, like Shakespeare's characters in disguise, have something to teach us about gender, sexuality, lived experience of difference and our relation to otherness.

In addition to telling stories of disguise and lived experiences of otherness, Queer theatre also recycles popular and traditional images, literature and narratives to critically comment and take claim to cultural materials they may normally be excluded from. We can see this in the works of Queer artists such as Split Britches and their reworking of *A Street Car Named Desire* entitled *Belle Reprieve* (1991), in the acts of Drag Queens and Kings and musical and television spoofs such as Diversionary Theatre's *Re-Designing Women,* a comedy queering of the 1980s hit American show *Designing Women.* Queer appropriation of cultural materials is an act of 'queering' (used as a verb) and serves several functions in the Queer community, to entertain, to challenge questions of 'normative' and to reposition queer stories in the traditional canon. Queering cultural materials is not limited to altering images of Marilyn Monroe, rewriting Madonna songs or spoofing *The Wizard of Oz*; it includes revisions of classical as well as contemporary literature, such as Shakespeare.

The plays productions discussed in this chapter all overtly queer Shakespeare. Some by foregrounding gay, lesbian and trans stories through directorial conceptual revisioning or by altering the work of Shakespeare. Moreover these plays have been queered through adaptation, reimagination and appropriation. Some tell whole new stories, recycling Shakespeare to pervert the classical 'traditional' narrative, rewriting LGBTQ experience into Shakespeare.

A Gay Island

One of the first gay appropriations of Shakespeare was based on a queering of Shakespeare's *The Tempest*. Philip Osmet's *This Island's Mine* was originally produced by the Gay Sweatshop Theatre Company in the UK as a staged reading in 1987 and was fully produced by the company in 1988. The company was originally founded in 1975 with the mission:

> To counteract the prevailing perception in mainstream theatre of what homosexuals were like, therefore providing a more realistic image for the public and to increase the general awareness of the oppression of sexuality, both gay and straight, the impact it has on people's lives and the society that reinforces it. (Malone *Unfinishedhistories.com* 2013)

This Island's Mine is considered Osmet's response to the oppressive conservative political landscape generated as Prime Minister Margaret

Thatcher held influence in Britain and was bringing forth laws such as Section 28 of the Local Government Act that were discriminatory to homosexual men and women (Fischlin and Fortier 2000: 255). The play borrows from Shakespeare's *The Tempest* to quench the playwright's 'desire to forge links between actual exiles and people who feel like exiles in their own country, as he himself did when he began work on it in the midst of the hysterical homophobia which marked the late 1980s' (Chedgzoy 1995: 2).

This Island's Mine uses a mix of narrative direct address speeches and dialogue to stage its queer reading. Although the play's title is in direct reference to Shakespeare's play, unlike other Queer plays discussed in this chapter, its links to *The Tempest* are 'deeper and more wide-ranging' (Fischlin and Fortier 2000: 255). This unique positioning occurs through the adaptation of themes and characters in the play, and the transposition of Prospero's 'colonization' of the Islanders, such as Caliban, and highlighting the oppressive politics at play on homosexuals in late 1980s America and the UK.

The play has traces of Shakespeare but presents more of an adapted new work than a reimaging of Shakespeare. Borrowing from The Bard, Osmet places the subject of 'a primary canon' that excludes minority narratives at the core of Queer questioning and, at the same time, creates a Queer classical canon that subverts the iconical status of the 'traditional' one. Osmet's play weaves several intricate stories together with a Shakespearean thematic backdrop. These stories present narratives of otherness and, as Bommer explains in the *Chicago Reader* (28 March 1996), include:

> a wide-eyed young gay man who seeks refuge with his homosexual uncle, a Jewish war refugee and her beloved cat, a young interracial gay couple fighting a hostile family, and a white lesbian couple with an intolerant son.

Similarly, many Queer Shakespeare plays and productions have approached Shakespeare through appropriation, restaging and rewriting because, as Kate Bornstein points out, 'Traditional form permits an audience to experience non-traditional content in relative safety' (1994: 150). This experience also ties back to Shakespeare's theatre if we consider that given 'the liminal nature of theatre', even in the Elizabethan era artists were able to stage actions and gender representations 'not typically permitted in normative society' (Lublin 2012: 68).

This Island's Mine toured throughout the UK but played to mostly LGBTQ audiences in the late 1980s. According to Silverstone's records

(2011) the play resonated with the unrest and discord experienced by members of the LGBTQ community and prompted them to take political action against discriminatory laws, such as section 28, and inequitable cultural practices. Almost 30 years later, Queer theatre companies and productions of Shakespeare are still working to broaden their reach beyond the LGBTQ community, whilst politically presenting queer stories. Queer artists face many of the same challenges as that of Philip Osmet and the Gay Sweatshop Theatre Company, albeit in evolving 'gay friendly' and pro-diversity cultures. Since *This Island's Mine* was first presented, new approaches to queering Shakespeare have been explored to address the changing political and cultural landscape. However, some hallmarks in these queerings remain – an emphasis on the presentation of 'otherness' and self-expressed identity, a foregrounding of underrepresented stories and figures and a theatrical revolt against mainstream practice and ideology.

Lesbians in Verona

Using Shakespeare's plays to present alternative lives and loves is part of an evolutionary Queer theatrical practice that has become increasingly popular as LGBTQ political struggles necessitate new platforms to voice an existence. Gay men and homosexuality were more prevalent in earlier movements, such as the 70s and 80s, but recently the shift has been on lesbian visibility as the copious number of lesbian reimagings of Shakespeare currently being staged proves.

In 2013 and 2014 several theatre companies purposefully staged 'lesbian' revisions of Shakespeare's *Romeo and Juliet*. {Your Name Here} A Queer Theatre in New York City staged *Juliet and Romeo* in coproduction at The Tank, June 2013. The production was the vision of Victoria Tucci and was directed and adapted by Mark Duncan. The concept for the production was to retell Shakespeare's classic story of star-crossed lovers for a modern audience by changing the gender of Romeo to female and altering the story from a heterosexual 'traditional' model to that of a homosexual one, featuring a lesbian love story:

> Set in modern day America we are building on the already existing themes in Shakespeare's text of hate, homelessness and suicide in order to explore this story through the lens of, 'what happens to queer youth when they are not given the support they need?' (Brownpapertickets.com 2013)

Like Gay Sweatshop, {Your Name Here} A Queer Theatre is a company with the aim of promoting Queer stories and making the LGBTQ community more visible through theatre, education and advocacy. *Juliet and Romeo* is just one production of many that borrows from the classical canon to reposition queer lives in historic and iconic literary works. *Juliet and Romeo* was produced in tangent with an LGBTQ campaign 'that tackles how we as a community can better support queer youth– focusing on issues such as suicide, homelessness, and hate crime in the LGBTQ community' ({Your Name Here} website 2014) and included a panel of guest speakers following the performances.

One year later, another lesbian *Romeo and Juliet* revisioned production entitled *The Deliverance of Juliet and Her Romeo* was staged at Unit 102 Theatre by the Leroy Street Theatre company in Toronto Canada, directed by Harrison Thomas. 'Using the words of Shakespeare to new effect' (Leroy Street Theatre website 2014), this adaptation is set in a small North American town with the conservatively religious Montagues and the 'cult' following Capulet family, at odds with one another and desperate to have their young girls 'procreate'. This adaptation captures the family tensions using the dramatic storyline that their 'daughters', Juliet and Romeo, fall madly in love despite their families' objections to their lesbianism. The play explores themes of not only familial bonds and homophobia, but also questions of religious indoctrination, segregation and teenage angst. The production also presented a mixed gender cast, including a female Mercutio played by Lauren Horejda and a Lady Capulet shared by three actors to reveal various interpretations of that role.

> This show's great strength is its multi-layered complexity. Thankfully, it doesn't slip into the comfortable territory most queer reimaginings of Romeo and Juliet fall into where the tragedy of the deaths of the title characters is told through the lens of queer tragedy. Instead, we're given a rich story of pain, grief, and extremism that is told through a uniquely queer lens. Although the central story of the romance between two women takes centre stage, it's tragedy is as universal as Shakespeare's telling of the story is thanks in part to the show's focus on its many other characters. (Gardiner *jeremythinksthings .wordpress.com* 2014)

This production succeeds as a Queer revisioning because it foregrounds lesbian experience through the adaptation of Shakespeare's text. Its experimental casting also aids the approach by widening the focus of the performance to include other characters in the story whilst revealing interesting interpretations to support the overall theatrical event.

Lesbian Shakespeare adaptations and revisions are not just found in North America. In 2012 Tallulah Theatre presented their 'it's a girl thing' lesbian all-female *Romeo and Juliet* production at the Bierkeller Theatre in Bristol. The community interest group, led by Louise Barrett and Tessa McGinn, aims to 'give lesbian and transgender women the opportunity to explore classic and modern texts that have been originally written to tell a heterosexual tale' (missinglesbians.co.uk 2012). In keeping with their aims, the production focused on the relationship between the two female lovers in an abridged version of Shakespeare's play and featured an all-female cast with a minimalist set. The production was also staged as part of the Brewhouse festival of works in progress and gained support from the local Arts Council as well as LGBTQ groups throughout Southwest England.

Although many of these productions find community support, raise social awareness and visibility for LGBTQ people and are received by the public positively, some productions have faced stern external criticism and artists have faced harsh, even threatening responses to their interpretation of Shakespeare. In 2001, a lesbian *Romeo and Juliet* staged at Birmingham's Crescent Theatre (UK) received heated critical opposition to the staging of the production, creating a controversy that gained national attention. Mediawatch UK representative Tony Wareing publically stated his position against the production. 'People are becoming heartily sick of this sort of thing being offered up as entertainment. What a pity we have to see this sort of sensationalism in an attempt to fill seats' (news24.com 2001).

Contrary to this assumption, the director's concept and non-traditional approach, including casting a 'homosexual transvestite' in the role of the Nurse, wasn't done to grab headlines. In response to this accusation, director Nick Fogg stated that the production 'is not meant to be offensive or gratuitous. It is being done carefully and tastefully in a modern setting, sticking faithfully to the original text' and added 'Romeo and Juliet is a love story, so in a modern context why shouldn't it be a story between two women or two men?' (*The Daily Telegraph* 23 July 2001).

As a result of the unique queering of Shakespeare and placing lesbian women at the centre of possibly Shakespeare's most popular tragedy, many of these productions grab the attention of not only the local community but national and international interest as well. In 2013, a small relatively unknown company gained international attention with their lesbian version of *Romeo and Juliet* not because of the queering of the production, but because of the unwarranted threats the artists received.

Before their *Romeo and Juliet* opened to the public, the producers of Curio Theatre Company in Philadelphia Pennsylvania received thousands of complaints, threats and hate mail in an effort to 'scare' the company out of producing the show.

In her article on the issue, Kirsten Koza calls the homophobic public 'the mob' and explains that part of the outcry by 'the mob' was in part due to the fact that the performance space occupied by Curio Theatre Company was the Calvary Center, formerly a church. She writes:

> The mob is mad that a lesbian 'Romeo and Juliet' is being staged in an old church. They probably don't know that Shakespeare's original text is sprinkled with homoeroticism and is performed in many converted churches. (*The Blot Magazine* 21 October 2013)

Some of the threats appeared on the 12 September 2013 *Philadelphia Magazine* web blog connected to a press interview with the artists on the upcoming production. The homophobic comments included Northwest Raised's 'Homeo and Juliet. Can't wait to miss it', Snowpersonable's 'The Methodist Church has fallen to a new low in an attempt to be "politically correct" in embracing and lending credibility to a lifestyle that offers nothing but shame and despair. Woe be unto those who call good evil and evil good' and Max Fisher's 'These people should be hunted down and killed.'[1] The company took all the threats, those on the web and otherwise, seriously, and increased security during their run.

What is equally shocking about this response to the lesbian production is that this negative response happened in Philadelphia, Pennsylvania. In terms of gay culture, Philadelphia was represented in the late 1990s as a 'gay mecca', almost to rival San Francisco or Palm Springs. This was due to the fact that Philadelphia was the setting for the popular hit show *Queer as Folk* (the American version) and the impression was that it was a liberal and safe haven for gays and lesbians. Despite radical outbursts to the contrary, Philadelphia, as a cosmopolitan centre, has a flourishing LGBTQ community and when the news broke about the resistances to the production, many community members attended and lent their support.

The political context in which the play was being staged in Pennsylvania was also a contributing factor to the homophobic responses. The play was positioned to tackle themes around 'gay marriage' and in the autumn of 2013 this was a hotly contested topic for

Pennsylvanians as conservatives in the state were fighting the Supreme Court ruling against the Defense of Marriage Act,[2] paving the way for gay men and women to legally marry. The ruling was limited to Federal recognitions of same-sex marriages and left state approvals for the states to battle individually. At the time of the production, strong arguments were being made for and against gay marriage as neighbouring states, such as New York, ruled in favour of gay marriage and were issuing marriage licences. By staging a lesbian *Romeo and Juliet* with 'gay marriage' overtones as a theatrical discourse, in the heart of Pennsylvania at a time of 'gay marriage' tensions, the company placed themselves (for good or for bad) in the eye of the storm.

Another US Queer production focusing on the gay marriage debate was staged in 2012 at the Oregon Shakespeare Festival. The production, entitled *The Very Merry Wives of Windsor, Iowa*, was a modern appropriation that borrowed characters, themes and textual extracts from Shakespeare's *The Merry Wives of Windsor* to tell a new story about fictional 'wives', lives and politics in Iowa, USA. The play was written and adapted by Alison Carey in an effort to place Shakespeare squarely in the 'gay marriage' debate through the genius setting of Windsor, Iowa, the epicentre of American politics. In 2012, Iowa was at the centre of the political storm as states wrestled with questions regarding gay rights and were legally deciding for or against same-sex marriage for its residents. Iowa is considered part of America's 'Heartland', positioned at the geographical centre of the country, and the launch location of presidential political campaigns known as the 'Iowa caucuses'. The caucuses are presidential party debates and conventions that start the political campaign trail wherein it is decided which candidates from each political party will run for presidential office and what campaigns they will champion.

In January 2012, the Iowa caucuses were held as the incumbent president Barack Obama launched his campaign to stay in office, whilst the Republican Party battled to find a candidate capable of challenging Obama's mass appeal. The Republican Party's campaign consisted of political platforms banning abortions and gay marriage in the USA. Iowa was additionally ripe for the gay marriage debate as it approved same-sex marriages in 2009. Playwright Carey draws upon Iowa's 2012 political landscape in her adaptation but does so by capturing the debate with her own unique 'spin' and yet retains the humour and heart found in Shakespeare's original play.

Carey's adaptation is a clear transposition of context from Shakespeare's play to a contemporary Windsor, Iowa. Sir John Falstaff becomes Senator John Falstaff and at the start of the play he has 'lost the Iowa caucuses and is deep in debt' and alights on an idea to increase his fiscal power by pursuing two women, Ford and Page, both of whom are 'married, one to a man, one to a woman. But in this heartland homeland, where gay marriage is legal and the state fair is about to open, hubris gets its comeuppance' (osfashland.org 2012).

The production was directed by Christopher Liam Moore and, like Curio's *Romeo and Juliet*, generated a mixed response from audiences and even critics such as Eric Minton of *Shakespeareances* (7 August 2012):

> We're not sure if the audience members who departed early in the first act were ultra-conservative, upset not only at the play's championing of same-sex marriage but also Falstaff's vague resemblance to Mitt Romney; or if they were ultra-liberals, bothered by the send-up of political correctness – after all, Annie 'comes out' as straight to her shocked parents after she elopes with Fenton.

Despite stories of walkouts during intermissions and some heated audience response, the play succeeded in updating Shakespeare's comedy and presenting challenging ideas in this bold, entertaining and very humourous adaptation.

> Shakespeare's play also has a couple of ridiculous subplots. Carey's adaptation makes them a bit them more convoluted still by throwing in same-sex relationships, marriage equality and the Iowa State Fair with its 600-pound sculptured butter cow. Not to mention topical political references, gay jokes just this side of offensive, rapid-fire wordplay, bad puns (are there any good puns?), slapstick humor and the traditional chase of bedroom farce. (*Daily Tidings Review* 27 June 2012)

New works through Queer positioning

As discussed Queer adaptations, appropriations and reimagings of Shakespeare are quite common, but fusion hybrids that mix theatrical and artistic styles tend to pointedly disrupt Shakespeare's text, whilst creating new works as part of a ShakesQueer canon. One such production was *The Verona Project* (2011) premiering at 'Cal Shakes', California Shakespeare Theatre in Berkeley California. *The Verona Project* was the brainchild of writer/director Amanda Dehnert. Dehnert (who also directed the OSF *Julius Caesar* discussed in the previous chapter) continues her legacy of experimenting with Shakespeare and gender. *The Verona Project*, however, is a departure from her staging of *Julius Caesar*, as it is not solely a regendering of Shakespeare's *Two Gentlemen of Verona* but also 'a hybrid of theater and live concert that marries Shakespeare to fairytales to real life, infusing it all with enough joyful exuberance to rock the Bruns to the imaginary rafters' (*calshakes.org* 2011). The play, or rather, performance event, uses a 'rock' show setting and the characters comprise a youthful, and sometimes conflicted, 'band', wrestling with their personal issues of self-expression and sexuality. The *Verona Project* does follow Shakespeare's narrative of boyhood friendship and the testing of bonds when it comes to affairs of the heart, but it also contemporises and departs from Shakespeare's text.

> Where it works best is in Dehnert's modernization of the old conflict between the claims of friendship and love as two young men begin to grow up. And in dumping the worst missteps (like the attempted rape) in Shakespeare's awkward first effort at comedy. Not to mention the joy of much of her eclectic score. (Hurwitt *San Francisco Chronicle* 11 July 2011)

The production is more akin to a rock musical than a classical play revision, possibly drawing upon other Queer tropes such as presented in *Hedwig and the Angry Inch* and *The Rocky Horror Picture Show*, and like these examples presents audiences with some gender swapping, both inherent in Shakespeare's text (Julia dresses as a boy in the original to pursue her lover Proteus) and re-imagined. In her article for *The Bay Citizen* (11 July 2011), Chloe Veltman praises the simple use of 'o' to mark the gender change of Shakespeare's Silvia to Dehnert's Silvio:

> By playfully using a simple vowel switcheroo to create a homosexual coming-of-age narrative that sees Valentine and Proteus vying for a male version of Silvia, Denhert imposes upon the play a nuanced vision of romantic love and self-knowledge that's reminiscent of the clever identity politics in later Shakespeare comedies like 'As you Like It' and 'Twelfth Night.'

The production was quite critically successful and even made the *New York Times* Summer Theatre list (5 May 2011), 'The director Amanda Dehnert ... is not a neophyte at retooling classics' proving that such 'projects' with Shakespeare can be engaging to audiences and critics alike.

Productions such as *The Verona Project* that borrow Shakespeare's narratives to tell new stories not only can refresh Shakespeare for seasonal subscription holders that may have seen a particular play presented traditionally too many times, but may also speak to 'next generation' audiences reflecting their lives and loves.

The Verona Project used social media, such as Facebook, to gather a younger audience, one that may not have normally attended Shakespeare. One such promotional tool was the creators' use of blogs to record the rehearsal and production process. Philippa Kelly, serving as resident dramaturg on the project, managed an interactive blog on the company website that prompted responses from her virtual audience. Her post on 27 June 2011 states, 'Every love is in its own way new, and yet as ancient as the sun and moon. Denhert and her cast take us on a trip through love and loss, using music as the wings to whisk us to heights of giddyness and delight', and then later asks:

> Are you going to see our production of *Verona*? Do you have questions or comments about the production's themes, creative choices, or anything else? Please leave them in the comments, and I'll be sure to respond.

The blog generated mixed responses, particularly as the play presented a 'gay' relationship not in Shakespeare's original text, but many remarked that they had taken someone younger, usually a teen, to the production 'to foster interest' in Shakespeare and live theatre. Although a few responses from parents seemed concerned about the content and presentation of a 'gay oriented social agenda' on the stage through Shakespeare, it was clear that the production succeeded in its reach to include younger audiences in the Shakespeare event.

Another work generated from a Queer positioning of Shakespeare's text is my own *Drag King Richard III*. The play is an appropriation of Shakespeare, borrowing extracts from Shakespeare's tragedy of *Richard III* to tell a new story about a lesbian friendship that is tested when one childhood friend transitions from being 'female' to 'male'. Written in 2003, the play is part Shakespeare, part autobiographical drama, and as such introduces a very personal perspective of the transgender experience told from the viewpoint of an ally, rather than from that of the person transitioning, which is most commonly presented in LGBTQ theatre.

The play is an important inclusion in the transgender canon and considered to be part of the early period of such plays presenting transgender identities and issues trans-men and women and others face in society. In his introductory speech at the audience question-and-answer session held at the Arnolfini in Bristol (2013), transgender scholar and activist Lazlo Pearlman explained that the play appears as an earlier work in the canon:

> As all of our communities have grown and changed and we have definitely had growing pains and it's been a rare occasion that we get to see some of those growing pains on stage in a respectful manner that takes in all sides of the debate and I am really excited that that is what this play has done.

Originally presented at the Edinburgh Fringe Festival by the Shakescene Players in 2004, the play has been produced by several theatre companies over the last decade including the Bristol Shakespeare Festival Theatre Company in 2013. Because of its complex subject matter, these companies often followed performances with open community discussions and question-and-answer sessions with audiences. The play works very well as a community engagement piece because the use of Shakespeare's text creates a foundation of legitimacy for the staging of a Queer narrative and performance experience. Oftentimes audiences drawn to the works of Shakespeare commingle in the theatrical space with queer non-traditional audiences, resulting in a unique exchange of thoughts and feelings.

At the 2013 Arnolfini performance, co-sponsored by the Bristol Shakespeare Festival and Bristol's We Are: Proud, audiences felt compelled to discuss the experience of watching the play and the issues it presented during the question-and-answer session. Sally Paskins, a former student of mine, openly praised the diversity of the audience: 'it's actually so nice that a play has actually conjured up such a diverse audience'; an older gentleman in his 60s responded the topical nature of the play, 'tonight is the first time I've understood what it's like to be transgendered'; and a younger man, taking the microphone from the panel of speakers felt inclined to comment upon the universality of the issues presented:

> There are so many really good themes to connect to for everyone and I've always told people that the trans story is everyone's story; that it is something that everyone can connect to. Everyone has friends that go away and come back transformed, whether that's through transitioning, coming out, or getting married and having children,

or going into the military. Those themes are what speak to your audience regardless of whether they're in a queer context or even more mainstream. (2013)

The diversity presented through the production also includes the representation of the actors as well. For example, the 2013 production featured transgender artist Joey Hately in the role of Laurie/Laurence/Richard and Hately served on the panel of transgender performance experts following the Arnolfini performance. In addition to Lazlo Pearlman, the panel also included trans-fiction writer Jack Wolf, director Roz Hopkinson, Hately's fellow actor Belle Jones and myself as playwright. Not only Hately's presence in the production helped to create a legitimised performance as a true trans experience and body was presented literally and figuratively for audiences, but Hately was able to draw out more current debates on the subject as significant trans perspectives and attitudes had changed since the play's inception in 2003.

Initially Hately was concerned about the possible paralleling between monstrousness and villainy, discussed in Shakespeare's *Richard III* text to that of the trans experience in the Laurie/Laurence/Richard III representation the play presents. Trans people have been vilified in the media for decades as 'monsters' and by 2013 were fighting to rewrite this stigma. Would the comparison to Shakespeare's Richard III further establish this myth? This was the question plaguing Hately's approach to the project. However, by focusing upon other aspects of the connection between Richard III and Laurie/Laurence the transgender character in the play new understandings of trans experience was highlighted and such associations were discussed in the post show panel. Hately's work to eradicate the negative association worked well, as his performance was convincing to audiences and critics such as Lou Trimby of *Bristol 24-7* (July 2013):

The dialogue taken from *Richard III* is apposite and effective when describing Laurie's loathing of her female and feminine body. Richard III was presented by Shakespeare as a hunched, twisted, deformed individual, not just physically but emotionally and psychologically. Possibly one of the greatest and most long lasting pieces of propaganda ever, as contemporary accounts attest to Richard being a decent king.

Where *Drag King Richard III* differs from the Shakespeare is that Laurie is able to address her self-loathing and change, physically. Her physical changes effect positive cerebral and emotional changes, she becomes Laurence and the person he/she was born to be. Richard III had no hope of such redemptive action, he was Richard Crookback and he was destined to always be Richard Crookback.

Although the 2013 production was largely a success, the frisson and fractures it generated within the transgender community and with wider audiences continued to be experienced in further productions.

In 2014, *Drag King Richard III* was restaged and recast in London by Stance Theatre Company. Stance Theatre Company is a UK-based community interest theatre company dedicated to the development of 'theatrical works that entertain, inform and stimulate dialogues with marginalised communities whilst also encouraging artistic and educational inclusiveness'. The company, of which I am a founding member, aims 'to create and test practical approaches with diverse audiences to change negative attitudes on topics or groups routinely silenced, discriminated against, vulnerable, or historically and/or culturally excluded' (*stancetc.wix.com* 2014) as part of our commitment to community engagement.

The London premiere of *Drag King Richard III* was held at The Riverside Studios July–August 2014 and, like the Bristol Shakespeare Theatre Company's Arnolfini event, all performances were followed with an expert panel discussion featuring key artists and scholars working on the production or in the field of transgender performance and politics. For example, the first set of post-performance discussions was facilitated by transgender activist and photographer Del LaGrace Volcano. The panel discussions with audiences were considered 'as fascinating as the play itself' (James *London City Nights* 30 July 2014) as Volcano's physical presence and performative readings 'about his experience as an intersex "hermaphrodyke"' (Czyzselska *Diva* 31 July 2014) challenged most of the audiences' preconceptions about gender whilst stimulating a starting point for an interactive discussion regarding the transgender experience. Later panel discussions were hosted by Laura Bridgeman transgender performer and author of *The Butch Monologues* and proved to be equally stimulating for audiences:

The Q&A audience were especially attentive to the play's status as more of (as one participant called it) 'a period piece', able to provide the first steps in informing audiences about trans* issues without necessarily capturing current development in trans* culture and politics. (Seymour *Exeunt Magazine* 3 August 2014)

The play's period and location, set in the late 1980s and early 90s in rural Georgia, USA, provided both a critical distance for London audiences and fodder for current transgender and gay rights debates. This unique positioning polarised not only audiences as they debated the value of staging a piece that is set in an earlier trans history, but the critics as well. A number of reviews praised the performance and its discussion sessions with artists. Chris Bridges of *Gay UK* (1 August 2014) wrote the 'award winning piece is a funny, deftly written play with some genuinely moving moments' and that it 'is much more than a straightforward "issues" play.' Max Sycamore for *London Theatre 1* (30 July 2014) declared that the production was 'easily one of the most thought-provoking shows on the London stage at the moment' and that the newly adapted 'script is fearless, featuring scenes packed with a brutal honesty that can only be applauded'. Conversely other critics took aim at the use of Shakespeare in a trans/gay themed play, disliking the fusion of the classical text with a more contemporary and personal narrative.

> The blocks of Shakespearean text are a bit like the ad breaks in an ITV drama, interrupting plot and stalling momentum. When Power tells the story of Laurie and La Femme it is deeply, deeply interesting. If I wanted *Richard III* I could have popped over to Trafalgar Studios instead. (Harrison *A Younger Theatre* 1 August 2014)

Despite their differences in opinions, the critics mostly agreed upon the poignancy of the production and the necessary dialogue it produced on the topic of gender, sexuality and performance:

> The play captures an important moment in the acceptance of LGBT+ people into 'mainstream' society. It shows that it was not so long ago, nor so far away, when coming out was an enormously difficult step to take. It also reminds us that in many parts of the world, it still is. (Naylor *Broadwayworld.com* 2014)

This was part of the conundrum created by the production and its post-performance discussion. Many LGBTQ members felt that the issues were dated, that we as a society have moved on from such narrow views of gender, whereas other audience members found the issues timely and still part of an ongoing dialogue. Non-LGBTQ audience members expressed that their experience of the play and the debates that followed eye-opening and revelatory. Often in the post-performance discussions political outrages were expressed at the fact that this particular story, of the countless multitudes on trans experience, was given support and staging, to which we could only surmise that such criticism within a community of mostly silenced authors is inevitable.

Despite some criticism from within the LGBTQ community, the queering of Shakespeare and infusion of a personal trans story in *Drag King Richard III* serves a very important function within the wider community. As a production the work brings diverse audiences together in a performance event that, like in so many of Shakespeare's plays, 'asks very big questions' (Dibdin *The Stage* 2004) about gender, identity and what it means to be human in a culture bent on defining us from birth. Queer stagings, revisions and appropriations of Shakespeare demand a new kind of reading encased in a classical form, and the productions often expose personal experiences of otherness to gain social and political presence. Like the work of Shakespeare, these productions are of their time and, as LGBTQ visibility and equality remains an issue in our culture, still relevant and timeless.

10
The Cross-Gender Workshop

This chapter introduces key practical considerations for deconstructing, analysing and regendering participants for cross-gender Shakespeare performance explorations. Although this volume focuses primarily on Shakespeare in practice, the exercises are derived from and can be applied to other types of gender performance. We will begin our practice-based study with a discussion of the workshop, its origins, practices and applications so we can better understand the theories and exercises that underpin the practical explorations. Later we will explore the exercises in depth, and you will be able to test them for yourself as you play with gender and Shakespeare. This process will aid you as you rethink gender and, possibly, construct your own performances, social or theatrical, publicly or for private aims.

I constructed the cross-gender workshop for artists in 2006 as part of my practice-based research when working with female performers attempting to embody masculinity in a variety of gender explorations, including that of Shakespeare's most famous male roles. Since that time, I have shared the workshop and exercises with students and professional artists of all genders, in mixed genres of performance, and have enjoyed the resulting outcomes.

The workshop and suggested exercises are based on several performance theories, methodologies and practitioners that I initially studied during my PhD research period 2004–2010. I worked to develop the workshop on my own, at first, testing exercises that best developed my extra-daily body for cross-gender performance and exploring theories and methods in practice and then later sharing my discoveries with students and artists, which became the basis of the cross-gender workshop. Early in the process I realised that the transformations needed to fully embody cross-gender roles would require extreme physical and vocal training over and above the demands already placed upon the actor when performing Shakespeare. Initially, I was drawn to several physical performance techniques and practitioners, such as introduced in the teachings of Jerzy Grotowski and Jacques Lecoq. However, it was the Japanese training techniques of Yoshi Oida and Tadashi Suzuki that formed the basis of this method in terms of a physical approach to cross-gender performance.

By implementing Japanese-based training techniques into my methodology for cross-gender performance, I seek to help actors develop their bodies into 'an 'object' that can be made more resonant and significant' (Oida and Marshall 1997: 37). The intense physical training allows the actors to become hyper-aware of how their bodies communicate gender to an audience. This acknowledgement is fundamental to maintaining the theatrical semiotics imposed by the act of playing across our 'natural' gendered state.

This rigorous training allows the actor to develop control over the nuances between the 'fixed' body and the 'fluid' articulation of gender and character, directing the audience's gaze and imagination from the seemingly 'fixed' to the fluid illusory performance of gender.

> For me, acting is not about showing my presence or displaying my technique. Rather it is about revealing, through acting, 'something else', something that the audience doesn't encounter in daily life. The actor doesn't demonstrate it. It is not physically visible, but, through the engagement of the onlooker's imagination, 'something else' will appear in his or her mind. (1997: Xvii)

Gender workshop history

Gender workshops primarily evolved out of feminist approaches to create events wherein women could discuss and explore issues of gender in society. These were sometimes called consciousness raising (CR) workshops as we discussed earlier in this volume. CR workshops evolved into gender performance workshops and were given more practical focus by theatre makers and applied drama specialists. In *Feminism and Theatre*, Sue-Ellen Case describes how the It's All Right to be Woman Theatre troupe used CR techniques along with movement and acting exercises in order to devise their feminist theatre productions:

These productions were a kind of public CR-group experience ... they could be perceived as dramatisations of the dynamics of the CR process: the productions used material from the women's experiences that had emerged in the CR process, and the audience acted like a kind of extended CR group that listened to the individual member articulate her experience of being a woman. (Case 1988: 65)

In past feminist theatre workshops, social and theatrical critiques of gender were cited to produce work that created a dialogue within the workshop, and even within resulting performances. However, these workshops focused upon women and feminine/female performances of gender and not sociological constructions and performances of masculinity or other gendered possibilities. Also gender workshops, such as led by the all-female Shakespeare companies discussed earlier, have focused upon the construction and performance of masculinity with female participants, but these workshops usually place emphasis upon the 'performance' of masculinity and neglect a focus on femininity and generally exclude men from participating. Additionally, these workshops generally are run like a 'how to' guide, and can sometimes leave the sociopolitical theoretical critiques for the scholars to analyse. My cross-gender workshop was conceived as a site wherein I might answer the research questions I posed as part of my PhD, test the knowledge and exercises I uncovered and share my growing methodology for performing many gendered roles in theatrical performance with other artists. The workshop also served to bridge the gap between these former workshop formats, bringing feminist theoretical critiques of gender construction and performance to theatrical explorations of genders, particularly that of cross-gender Shakespeare.

Jill Dolan in her book *Presence and Desire: Essays on Gender, Sexuality, Performance* writes about the importance of such explorations and transactions for the theatre:

The performance of gender is a crucial concept in contemporary feminist thinking, as it has been conceptualized by thinkers such as Judith Butler and Theresa de Laurentis as well as other scholars in the burgeoning field of gay and lesbian studies. The performance of gender in everyday life is now being carefully denaturalized in these writings, but performance in theatre remains a place where feminist theory can be tested and enacted. (Dolan 1999: 100)

The cross-gender workshop is based upon a feminist approach and analysis of gender and borrows early and current feminist workshop and CR experiences and practices to discuss and explore gender in a safe setting. However, this workshop explores all genders theatrically and aims to include all people in the workshop dialogue. After all, Shakespeare presents multifarious characters and gender performance layers, and the workshop should reflect and support such performances.

Constructing gender: A Brechtian approach

Unlike the acting approach to building character described by Konstantin Stanislavsky that is essentially based in psychological realism in the cross-gender workshop we employ a Brechtian approach, building our characters from a sociological viewpoint. This viewpoint is not solely constructed by the actor's imagination, as is instructed in Stanislavsky's method, but rather in constant negotiation and consort of opinions and experiences shared by the collection of participants in the workshop. Brecht writes about this sociological approach to creating character's for the stage in *Brecht on Theatre*:

> When the actor comes to examine the truth of this performance – a necessary operation, which gives Stanislavsky a lot of trouble – he is not merely thrown back on his natural sensibility. He can always be corrected by reference to reality. Does an angry man really speak like that? Does a guilty man sit like that? He can be corrected, that is, from without, by other people. (Brecht 1964: 33)

How Brechtian sociological method to building character is used in the workshop can be most easily identified in the approach we use to examine our own social presentations of gender and then apply similar critiques for building personas and Shakespeare's characters. We begin the workshop as ourselves wearing our clothing, make-up, jewellery, and so on, as we would in 'every day' life. We then move into a discussion of how the gender binary is at play in our society and map out cultural gender 'rules' for men and women as prescribed to us based upon our 'sex'. The gender map forms a very specific sociological guide that reflects our culture, time and fashionable approaches to gender.

Having worked with international artists from across many cultures, I have to state that gender rules can vary greatly from one country or region to another. Gender mapping is integral to the process of our understanding of what 'defines' men and women in the culture we are performing 'to' in the 'here and now'. Being culturally specific means that we can reflect or reject those rules in front of our 'audience'. The audience will also recognise those rules, actions and behaviours that you ultimately adopt, adapt or reject.

After the initial introduction, discussions of social gender programming and our gender mapping session, we participate in self-observation exercises. This facilitates a discussion about how we 'perform' our genders and aids us to discovering what we need to address as we attempt to 'become' a gender other than our 'natural' or 'normative' one. Once we have gone through this process, the workshop moves into a more practical focus. I introduce preparatory techniques for 'neutralising' the body's gender signifiers. Before attending the workshop the participants have been instructed to begin by wearing their own attire but also to bring kit to change into as instructed. I have two reasons for requesting this: to allow participants the opportunity to critique their own performance of gender, as would be highlighted in the acts of wearing their own clothes, and then to give them a sense of 'neutral' through the wearing of non-gendered attire to experience a sense of ungendering, which acts as a starting place to layer on 'other' genders. We document these transformations through before and after still photographs, so later we can more easily comment on the overall experience of 'gendering'.

At this stage the participants and I often discuss how the simple act of changing into our neutral kit already serves our intention to suppress our 'natural' genders and (particularly for women) to 'refuse the gaze', aiding in our transformation from being 'objects' to 'subjects' and, then finally, 'producers of meaning'. The basic loose black kit makes us less gender defined (androgynous), and we begin to discover 'a state of readiness', a neutral or rather preparatory state that quiets our personal gender performance and, upon which, we can layer new gender signs. Patsy Rodenburg explains that in the state of readiness 'The energy is efficiently centered in the breath and the breath support. All options are available – neither too relaxed (although you can appear relaxed) nor too tense' (Rodenburg 2002: 23). This is an important state for performing Shakespeare and playing with gender. Also the state of readiness can be likened to 'between-ness', 'nothingness' or 'becoming' as is described in Eastern practices such as butoh dance.

It is from this state of readiness that the actor can suppress personal gender semiotics, which may limit imagination, in order to adopt 'other' gender acts. This state is an essential component to performing cross-gender roles and aids the actor's transformation from 'self' to 'Other'. Rhonda Blair writes about the benefits of cross-gender performance and actors identifying with an 'Other':

> Cross-gender work requires the actor to identify with a seeming Other, imagine what it must be like to be the Other, and break years of physical, vocal, and emotional conditioning in order to perform that Other. (1993: 297–298)

This experience is primarily the main practice goal for the first day with participants. I aim to help them experience this state and be able to return to it so that they may 'playfully put on and take off the gendered sign systems of appearance' (Aston 1995: 103).

Once we discuss and explore the state of readiness, I expand upon their experiential understanding of this state through the use of yoga and Suzuki exercises that are highly psycho-physical. Although the exercises are very technical and can be difficult to master, the physical discipline aids the entire cross-gender process. We also use a series of *katas* in order to further develop our physical discipline and understanding of how gender is performed. The series of *katas* and powerful movements introduced to participants serve to 'free-up the body, contrary to the way in which they have been "instructed" to be restrained, constrained by experience of their engendered socialization' (1995: 99). We will discuss *katas* in depth in the next section.

Another aim of such physical exercises is to give the participants an opportunity to experience the *hara* in practice. Used in many forms of Asian martial arts, spiritual and theatrical practice, the *hara* holistically connects the body, mind and spirit as one unit. Many Western practices refer to this area as 'the core', centre or belly. It is located a few inches below the navel, and when working with new actors (particularly women) I usually request that they wear a loose hanging belt with a big buckle to help indicate the *hara* throughout our work. Lorna Marshall helps to describe the *hara* further: 'the Japanese concept of the *hara* is seen as something more than a physical location; it is the core of the entire self. It is the centre of a person's strength, health, energy, integrity, and sense of connection to the outside world and the universe' (Oida and Marshall 1997: 10). This is an important step in the process of cross-gender performance, as many young artists tend not to work from their core and never experience how to shape their performances with the central power needed to sustain long physical and vocal performances demanded in the works of Shakespeare.

Another source of connection to the world and universe that I use in our psycho-physical explorations is an emphasis on the feet. As we work with physical and *hara* awareness, we remain barefoot, establishing our connection to the earth through the soles of our feet. I ask participants to 'breathe through their feet' and this assists them to breathe more deeply. In this approach, I use several simple Suzuki exercises, such as walking and stamping of the feet to build the connection between breath and body. Tadashi Suzuki suggests, 'There are many cases in which the position of the feet determines even the strength and nuance of the actor's voice' (Suzuki 1986: 6). Also, in the case of stamping the feet, a performer begins to feel their power through the relationship between her breath and body. Another key benefit of stamping the feet is that 'It is a gesture that can lead to the creation of a fictional space, perhaps even a ritual space, in which the actor's body can achieve a transformation' (1986: 12).

Dolan writes about discovering this essential point in her own cross-cast production: 'Gender reads as a relation – of parts of the body to the whole, of bodies to one another, of the body to its context' (1999: 109). Each actor must understand all of these relations as part of their performance and how they will shift and change throughout the narrative depending upon dynamics of class, power, and so on, introduced through the storyline or characters that are interacting with the primary actors.

Rodenburg describes in *Speaking Shakespeare* that the body of Shakespeare's time was experientially different from today. At any moment, a man may have to fight to the death, and this was a constant reality as swords were worn by men – part fashion, part function. This dramatic atmosphere was embodied in the people of the Elizabethan era. They were constantly in a 'state of readiness', a state wherein they were ready for any and all possible actions. She then describes how modern actors may understand this state: 'The readiness that I am describing is a physical state of vivid alertness and presence that matches the heightened awareness and imagination of the Shakespearean character at this moment' (2002: 23). Developing the artist's heightened state of psycho-physical awareness throughout the workshop is one of the main aims of this approach, and such awareness aids actors in their physical and vocal gendered performances when exploring cross-gender roles.

Introducing *Katas*

As I discussed, this work is based upon cultural gender stereotypes, and we discover in the workshop that our personal experiences and expressions of gender do not fit to the far right or far left of the gender spectrum. We often find that we are somewhere between or that the gender stereotypes dictated by society have no basis in real experiences of gender. This is generally an 'aha' moment for many.

However, our audiences have a 'cultural' map that they refer to when attending our performances or, indeed, watching our social performances as we walk through the world. The gender map is based upon cultural stereotypes which are important for us to identify and interrogate. Anne Bogart explains this point in the chapter on stereotypes in her book *A Director Prepares*:

> A stereotype is a container of memory. If these culturally transmuted containers are entered, heated up and awakened, perhaps we might, in the heat of the interaction, reaccess the original messages, meanings and histories they embody. (2001: 95)

Understanding the history of cultural stereotypes and how they act as containers for memory is a theorised and practical focus of our sessions as we perform *katas*. Keeping stereotypes in the forefront of our discussions, we can impart these ideas in our practice by using them physically as containers of form, such as through the creation of Japanese *katas*. *Katas* have been practised by and for the performance of both genders and act as a container for our first gendered performance explorations.

Katas are integral to Japanese performance and training techniques. They have become foundational conventions that define and articulate gender performance on the stages of Japan for centuries:

> The Japanese use the word kata to describe a prescribed set of movements that are repeatable ... In executing a kata, it is essential never to question its meaning but through the endless repetition the meaning starts to vibrate and acquire substance. (2001: 101)

As *katas* (used also in the martial arts, cooking, calligraphy, etc.) are clearly prescribed and repeatable they are no doubt reflective of the performance of gender. *Katas* embody the same theoretical supposition as Judith Butler's gender performativity theory:

> Gender is the repeated stylization of the body, a set of repeated acts within a highly rigid regulatory frame that congeals over time to produce the appearance of substance, of a natural sort of being. (Butler 1999: 44)

This is perhaps why they have been used to convey gender throughout Japanese theatrical history and associations with the traditions, such as Kabuki, can be easily applied to cross-gender Shakespeare.

In our practical rehearsal sessions I generally divide the group into smaller focused gender groups to work on constructing gender *katas* collaboratively. Participants in their groups construct a *kata* (or physical movement score) that is stereotypically gendered, physically identifiable as the gender being performed (such as a mother nursing a baby), and that can be simply adopted by any member of the group, repeated, and perfected. Once we have rehearsed these in the groups and they are mastered by each member, we perform them to all the participants of the workshop.

Similarly to the Brechtian example, we discuss the performance: questioning if it is stereotypical to the gender, asking how it might best convey the gender and how we might disrupt the gender performance if that is our aim. We interrogate the practice collectively and then return to create further and more intricate *katas* building upon what we've learned through our sharing of the *katas*.

In our rehearsal practice we use *katas* as a physical means to quiet individual gender and identity programming and articulations. These *katas* also serve to train the actors' physical abilities and body-mind connection. I focus our pre-performance work on *katas* such as the balancing and kicking kata to heighten the actor's sense of individual physical prowess and collective kinaesthetic awareness. We discover, through the endless repetitions, that these forms, although seemingly restrictive and identical in execution, convey performative subtleties and develop intensity of focus.

Anne Bogart explains, 'Paradoxically, it is the restrictions, the precision, the exactitude, that allows for the possibility of freedom' (2001: 46). In this process the internal performance of the actor is foregrounded through the repetitive restrictions of the external form. The actor can imagine that they are the Other, and their physical embodiment expresses a new gendered expression.

Cross-gender performance workshop: Practice guidelines

The gender map

If you are working in a group it is good to start with an open discussion of gender and how we are socially programmed to perform our gender. This discussion could start with a review of this topic as introduced in the 'In Theory' section of this book. I would suggest moving from this discussion to mapping out how the gender binary works and what the gender rules are in your culture.

When I create these maps I start by drawing a line on a chalk-board, smart board or large piece of paper and on the far right I write 'Masculine/Male/Man' and to the far left of the line I write 'Feminine/Female/Woman' and in the centre of the line I write 'Androgyny'. This creates a visual picture for participants to see how the binary gender-ing process works to identify gender differences in a patriarchal cul-ture wherein power and privilege is given to men and such distinctions between men and women are made.

We then start to discuss how we might physically identify if someone is male. Here you can refer to magazines, ads, movies, TV and other cul-tural materials. The question to ask is 'how do we read gender?' or, more specifically, 'what are the semiotics of masculinity?' Possible answers that are given might be 'men are tall, big, take up space, have large hands and feet' and I would write that down under the 'Masculine/Male/Man' side of the paper creating a column of identifying gender markers. Then we do the same for women. If men are tall, larger in stature, and so on, women are (as dictated by binary positioning) short, small and generally the direct opposite. Of course, we discover that this is not 'naturally' true, more likely a cultural ideal and stereotype, but it's part of a conditioning process in our culture for it to be perceived as true.

Discussions may arise about how men and women attempt to change their physical bodies to become larger or smaller and so on. The physi-cal lists are usually pretty long but we can also look at other attrib-utes as well, such as men are supposed to show little emotion, whereas being 'emotional' is considered a 'feminine' trait. This process creates the gender map, which is the basis for the cross-gender performance work. Once you construct your map, you can begin suppressing your gender performance and play up the attributes of the other gender. You can find ways to practically apply the traits and appearance of the other gender. For women, this usually means taking up more space as they sit, stand and move about the room. They might play more aggressively in games, be more voiced in their opinions and thoughts and wear facial hair. Men usually discover how to make their bodies smaller, creating curves rather than angles, gesturing from the heart or face, wearing make-up, and being more introspective and sensitive. This is all a great starting place for the overall workshop process and can generate very interesting performances even at the start of the workshop.

1.0 Preparation Process

1.1 Self-observation

Wearing your own clothes, and being and behaving as you do in your everyday life – observe yourself in a mirror. What do you look like at first glance, second and third? What do you immediately see and read in context to gender? What are you wearing? Record your thoughts. Make a video of yourself in space, moving, sitting, dancing, speaking and so on. Take photographs. Referring to the gender map, what masculine/feminine traits do you have already? What masculine/feminine traits might you have to hide in order to regender your appearance?

1.2 Gender Workshop

What do you qualify as masculine and feminine? What are their differences and how are those differences read in spatial relationships, through body language and mannerisms, through material and physical semiotics? Look at language and voice and think about how gender is indicated in our voice, in pitch, placement and the words we choose. Deborah Tannen (1990) covers this in the 'Genderlects' section of her book. Look at consumer culture, body fashioning and power dynamics. How are these aspects similar/different between cultures? Look at 'other' genders and in particular 'trans' gendered people. What do they tell us about gender performativity?

1.3 Research

Look into the history of women playing men and men playing women. Read *Transgender Warriors*, *Gender Outlaw*, and *Colonel Barker's Monstrous Regiment*. Research the beginnings of Kabuki theatre, Shakespeare's boy players and the Victorian 'breeches parts'. Read about Vesta Tilly and the female impersonators of the music halls and vaudeville era as they are often overlooked. Look at the cross-gender performances by men and women in the cabaret and dada movements.

Look at the reviews written about Sarah Bernhardt's *Hamlet*, Kathryn Hunter's *Richard III* and Fiona Shaw's *Richard II*. Rent some good movies like *Tootsie, Breakfast on Pluto, Victor/Victoria, Boys Don't Cry* and *TransAmerica*. Flip through the transgender site hosted by the XX Boyz and check out RuPaul's *Drag Race* and photography by Lauren Cameron. See a Drag King or

Queen performance, and if there isn't one nearby rent documentaries on the subject such as *Venus Boyz* and *Wigstock*. See a Shakespearean play like *As You Like It, Two Gentlemen of Verona* or *Twelfth Night*. Do your homework. Learn about the legacy cross-gender performers from the past have left us.

Research can also focus on specific character research for your role. When working on a Shakespearean character, you will want to conduct research on the period in which the play originated. What were the prevailing thoughts on gender and what were the gender expectations that may have influenced Shakespeare's writing. Think also in depth about the fictional culture and gender expectations in which your character lives. How does growing up as a teenager in Verona Italy differ from growing up there today? How does Juliet's gendered experience differ from that of Romeo's in *Romeo and Juliet*? What are the expectations, dress codes, rules of conduct and behaviour for these teens, and how are they expressed in the play's plot? How might you express these in your own performance? This research will prove invaluable once you start to construct your character later in the process.

1.4 Undo Your Gender

Change into black gender-neutral attire; loose-fitting/oversized tops and trousers work well. Always work with barefeet in preparatory stages. Take off all jewellery, make-up, hats and accessories. Tie long hair back in a tight bun or wear it back in a bandanna; just get it out of your way so it doesn't remind you of *you*. Allow yourself to feel different, to experience 'something else'.

1.5 Sacred Space

Find a 'sacred space' in which to work. Leave all outside thoughts outside the room. Leave your shoes and socks out there also. Make the room special. Burn incense and play soothing music. Give yourself full licence to explore, to laugh and to be serious if needed. Focus in approach is imperative to this work.

2.0 Finding Neutral

2.1 Begin with Breath

Work towards breathing fully and deeply into the *hara*. Stand with your feet more than hip distance apart and let your hands hang loose at your sides. Stand straight and tall, elongating the spine. Do not fidget; let go of feeling self-conscious; it has no place in this room. Close your eyes and focus on your internal processes. Relax. Breathe in through the nose and out through the mouth. Imagine breathing through the feet. Breathe out and pause before breathing in. Concentrate on the moment between breaths. Use the breath of fire yoga technique:

Breathe in through the nose rapidly, pause a moment and out through the nose rapidly. Try to pause when you have fully exhaled, breathe in through the nose again rapidly, pause and this time release the breath whilst making a 'Ha' sound. Repeat.

2.2 Physically Warm

Warm up the body so that it can relax and be fully stretched and prepared for work, through isolation stretches beginning with the head and moving downwards to the feet. Use the Suzuki 'grammar of the feet' exercises:

Walk around the space (or alternatively if in a group, walk in a circle) focusing your awareness in your feet. Massage the feet and rub them into the surface of the floor, using the toes, ball, heel, and so on. Then after a few minutes, lift the legs with knee bent high in front of the body and keep foot flexed, so that the upper thigh is parallel with the floor as well as the foot. Hold for two seconds and lightly stomp the foot flat to the floor. It is important here that the foot is perfectly flat and commanding the ground through the stomp. Switch legs and move about in this way for two minutes. Next change the way the foot contacts the floor in the stomp, such as coming down into contact on the toes, then heels, outside and inside of feet. This exercise should take up to ten minutes and it is important to keep the rest of the body neutral with hands at sides during the work.

2.3 Yoga Technique

Although most yoga practices and sequences could work equally as well, I introduce Astanga Vinyasa yoga at this point in the work. The sequence that I use most is a variation on the basic Astanga Vinyasa sequence. Starting in Downward Facing Dog position (inhale) and move into Plank position (exhale). From Plank, inhale and move slowly into Chaturanga on an exhale. Inhale as you move into cobra and exhale to Downward Facing Dog. For reference read *Astanga Yoga & Meditation*.

From this sequence I add an additional sequence as execution and strength develops. From Downward Facing Dog, inhale and jump your feet to your hands. Exhale whilst slowly moving to standing position one vertebrae at a time. Inhale as the hands and arms come over the head and into prayer position in front of your torso near chest. Exhale and reverse the direction of the hands as the body bends from the waist (Swan Dive forward) and folds over legs. In an inhale, stretch the torso forward and parallel to the floor (halfway up the body) and elongate the spine. Exhale and fold the torso into the legs again and let the hands fall by the feet. Place the hands firmly on the floor, inhale and step back or jump back into Downward Facing Dog and begin sequence again.

3.0 Technical Training for the Work

3.1 *Hara* Training Exercises

There are many *hara* exercises that I use throughout the training period.

This is a list of a few that I use most often:

The Roll-up

I will usually begin with the roll-up and introduce the use of a drum here. The participants then roll up and down the body on the floor to the beat of the drum. The starting position is to lie on the floor with your front facing up and completely stretched out with arms over head. The feet should be flexed not pointed and *hara* engaged working the entire time. As the drum beats, the arms rise up and towards the feet and slowly the body follows, moving upwards to seated position one vertebra at a time. Once the hands and arms are up and over the feet and legs, reverse the direction with control and emphasis in the *hara*. The teacher/drummer can pause, making the participants freeze at any time in the roll-up and the more difficult these pauses, the more developed the students' connection to their *hara* will be.

Suzuki Floor Positions

First position is the body in a ball. Second, the head and feet come up and are held by the *hara*. Third position, the legs, held together, come out and are held above the floor suspended by the *hara* and the arms pull back with fists at sides. Fourth position, the legs are spread and held suspended above the floor by the *hara* until the drum strikes and then the positions are reversed or changed up as directed by instructor. For further instructions read Suzuki's (1986) *The Way of Acting.*

Suzuki-Inspired Squats

Standing with the legs spread fairly wide and feet pointed out at an angle, the participants should execute a squat with torso upright and with legs parallel to the floor. This should be done to the beat of the drum, or within a count, such as five down, and then reversed for five up, returning to full standing position. Then each participant should rise slowly up onto their toes. The legs should still be spread wide and inner thighs should squeeze as though there was a ball between their legs. This action is then reversed back to standing. The participants should then alternate between the squats and the toe lifts. The hands are held in loose fists by the sides.

Suzuki Slow Motion Walk

Standing with legs slightly bent and with feet together facing forward, the participants slowly shift their weight unto their left leg whilst the right begins to rise. The rising leg should be bent and lifted until the upper thigh is parallel with the floor. The foot on the lifted leg should be flexed. The leg is then brought back to its starting position very slowly except that the foot should fit into the bridge of the left foot. It looks as though the right foot is only inches ahead of the left. The weight is shifted to the right leg and the sequence starts again with the left leg. This exercise should be done extremely slowly and the participants should not actually travel far in their walk. The hands are held in loose fists by the sides.

3.2 Physical Training Exercises

Katas are concentrated on in this section of the training. This allows the participants to learn the form, practise balance, build psycho-physical awareness and strengthen the *hara*, the body and mind.

Balancing Kata

Beginning position is similar to Suzuki slow-motion walk. Once the leg is lifted parallel to the floor position, it is extended (straightened) forward. It is then returned to the bent-knee position and then there is a shift of the pelvis and the bent leg is moved in position to the side of the performer. The leg is then extended out, parallel to the floor (like a side kick), and then brought back to bent position. At this point the entire sequence is reversed until the leg is brought back to the starting position and then there is a weight shift and the sequence begins again with the opposite leg. The hands are held in loose fists by the sides.

Kicking *Kata*

This *kata* involves a series of martial arts kicking moves. I use a sequence that begins with a prep before the kick and then starts with the right and alternates between the right and left legs. I begin with a straightforward travelling kick (right then left), forward travelling side kicks (right then left), roundhouse kicks (right then left), a bent leg lift (right then left) with a light stomp and a final foot stomp with both legs meeting in the end.

Gender *Katas*

Both roles involve codified movements beginning with seated bows, floor to standing rises, walks, pointing and seeing, descents to floor and sleeping positions. Each role should be explored by the artist to help them gain an understanding of how to perform gender in a codified form. This can be devised by the group if needed.

The gender *katas* should be simply structured and demonstrate clear physical and movement differences between the male and female roles. The male roles generally lead all movement and are strong with sweeping gestures, and movement takes up space and the foot is presented as heel to toe when contacting the floor. The female roles in kata form generally follow the male through the movement, legs are held together from knees up, rounded soft movements are physicalised, eyes look down to the floor whilst head floats lightly, and the foot is presented as toe to heel as it makes contact with the floor.

3.3 Gender and Bodily Movement Exercises

In this area of the training I introduce a wide variety of exercises that address physical articulations of gender in relationship with an audience and space.

Body Yin/Body Yang Exercise

The Chinese theory of yin-yang (in Japanese *in-yo*) holds that oppositions coexist in all phenomena – dark–light, soft–hard, weak–strong, female–male, and so on, through every quality one can imagine. No value is attached to yin or yang qualities. Nor is a choice made between one or the other. Zeami advises the actor–producer to find the appropriate balance between them. If one or another quality appears to be interesting, that is because it is experienced in conjunction with its opposite. (Brandon 1998: 105)

Begin in a neutral position and then move about the room as gender-neutrally as possible whilst also focusing on the feet. Move about the space and put awareness into your feet, thinking with the bodymind about the feet and the experience of moving the feet about the space and making contact with the floor. Then begin to feel yin energy in the feet and let that energy be expressed in just the feet without any other bodily movement. After a few minutes, switch focus and think about yang energy, begin to feel the yang energy in the feet and express it in your feet. After a few minutes, return to the 'neutral' still movement.

This exercise continues like this by gradually moving up the body section by section. I begin with the feet and move into the calves, then the upper thighs, the hips, the belly, the back, the chest, shoulders, arms, hands and face. Eventually the whole body of the performer is able to express yin and yang qualities and experience how each part can be isolated or combined in the performance of gender.

Gesture and Gender Exercise

Standing still and using music as inspiration, choose two gestures that are stereotypical or could be labelled as masculine and or feminine and perform them both physically with the body. Begin with the first gesture and use the whole body to over-articulate the gesture. Then move the whole body in a sweeping transition into the second gesture, also over-articulated with the whole body. Spend some time playing with these gestures by moving between them fast, slowly and still, as well as over-articulated at 100%, articulated at 50% and under-articulated at 25% effort.

Frozen Poses and Gender Exercise

Walking around the space, with inspirational music playing, find moments when you can stop and adapt a whole-bodied physical pose that articulates a male character from your imagination. Relax and walk again thinking about another male character. Imagine him in your mind. When you have a clear image of him and how he moves, stop again and create another pose that visually represents him. Do this for several minutes and record the work or take mental notes about the poses/characters that you found most interesting and/or visually striking.

Frozen Poses and Adjective Exercise

Like the exercise above, you should be walking about the space and creating character poses, but this time as you do you will voice an adjective that you feel describes your pose and/or character, for example, 'powerful', 'angry', 'sexual', 'royal', and so on. Play with this exercise for a bit until you gather two good poses and adjectives. Stand still, as in the exercise above, and move between these two poses and adjectives. Once you feel comfortable and relaxed, assume pose one and using this pose's adjective as a starting point, begin an improvised speech as your character that either starts with the adjective as the first word or the topic of the speech.

Your movement can then depart from the pose to organic movement inspired by the emerging character from your imagination. Try the same with the other movement. You can also expand on this exercise and use it to create different characters or incorporate more poses and challenge yourself by trying to include all poses and adjectives or (words and phrases) into one improvised character monologue. Later you can add lines from the play that you connect to and assist you in feeling closer to the gender, sociological and psychological experience of your character. For example, in Act 2 Scene 1 of *Julius Caesar* Portia vocally and textually references her place as a woman and as a wife, as she pleads with Brutus to share his woes:

> Is Brutus sick? and is it physical
> To walk unbraced and suck up the humours
> Of the dank morning? What, is Brutus sick,
> And will he steal out of his wholesome bed,

To dare the vile contagion of the night
And tempt the rheumy and unpurged air
To add unto his sickness? No, my Brutus;
You have some sick offence within your mind,
Which, by the right and virtue of my place,
I ought to know of: and, upon my knees,
I charm you, by my once-commended beauty,
By all your vows of love and that great vow
Which did incorporate and make us one,
That you unfold to me, yourself, your half,
Why you are heavy, and what men to-night
Have had to resort to you: for here have been
Some six or seven, who did hide their faces
Even from darkness.

In the speech, she feminises herself in her approach with Brutus, kneels before him and attempts to use her beauty to persuade him. She reminds him of their marriage vows that they are to be equals, 'your half' and as one but expresses that she feels that presently this is not so. His actions make her feel less than equal, and moreover, stating later in the scene, as though 'Portia is Brutus' harlot, not his wife.' A male actor working on this speech could incorporate a kneeling pose or *kata* with a pleading tone whilst asking 'Is Brutus sick?' and 'upon my knees, I charm you' to discover Portia's use of her femininity to 'heal' her husband and their marriage. Later adding the 'harlot wife' line might reveal even more psychological and emotional layers to the role. Many of the actors I have worked with have found this approach to be a great warm-up tool to inhabiting their characters just before entering the stage even after they have fully rehearsed and fleshed out their roles for performance.

4.0 Building Character and Gender Performance

4.1 Character Study

If the performer is creating an original character or character not fully fleshed out in Shakespeare's text, then I introduce a character study at this stage of the process. I ask participants to write out a biography for the character written in first person. This should encompass major events in their life, particularly rites of passage and gendered experiences. What was growing up in their family like? What expectations were made on them? What toys did they play with? Who were their friends and what adventures did they have? What was puberty like for the character? Did they have lovers? What profession did they go into? And so on. If a character grew up in a particular time period or place, we do research around this and allow that study to influence our explorations of character.

4.2 Character Questions

If the performer is creating a character based upon a text they can still apply some of the aspects of the character study using their imagination coupled with what they are given in the script and they will find the character questions a good source for building their character as well.

This is also a good time to comb the text for clues defining your character and the relationship he/she has with other characters in the play. What does their wife/husband say about them when they are in the room? When they are out of earshot? What does your character say about their husband/wife, child, mother or father and so on. How does your character's status change with certain characters? What lines give you clues about their feelings about others and other characters' feelings about you? Make sure to think about how all of these clues can be made actionable and be performed when in moments with other characters.

4.3 Character-Based Movement

In my workshops I use many exercises that allow the performers to imaginatively move and interact as their characters without speaking. These exercises help the performers physicalise their performance and give them an opportunity to play and interact as their characters and in their newly formed genders. These improvised exercises include giving them basic tasks and scenarios to explore walking, dancing, sitting, shaking hands, rough play, drinking, flirting, fighting, and so on. Usually I pair the performers up and play music so they can lose their inhibitions in their playing. Sometimes I separate them into two lines and have them greet in the centre of the space and then walk down the middle. If you are working on a particular Shakespeare scene or play, it often is very enlightening to borrow from the text to set up your imagined scenario. For example, if working on

Romeo and Juliet you might set up a ballroom improvisation with music and setting (even suggestive costuming at this stage) to allow the actors to interact in their cross-gendered roles, focusing upon gender rules for behaviour in your 'Verona' and changing social statuses amongst partygoers.

These exercises result in bodily articulations, gestures, interactions and free and unique movements. As they become more comfortable we improvise with texts and storylines aloud, creating short scenes as the characters. We rehearse these and then share them with the whole group for feedback. There are no rules here, but the more play is allowed and explored, the better the performance of gender becomes.

Part III

Debate and Provocation

11
Interview with Lisa Wolpe

Lisa Wolpe is an international activist working for the empowerment of women and diversity on the stage. Since 1993 she has been the Founding Producing Artistic Director of the award-winning all-female Los Angeles Women's Shakespeare Company (LAWSC). Where she produces, directs, and has performed roles including Hamlet, Richard III, Angelo, Leontes, Romeo, Shylock, and Iago. Lisa is currently touring her solo show "Shakespeare & the Alchemy of Gender" to venues around the world. She has directed and acted regionally at theaters including Oregon Shakespeare Festival, Colorado Shakespeare Festival, Berkeley Repertory Company, Shakespeare & Company, Arizona Theater Company, and San Diego Repertory Theater. She has received multiple awards for excellence in Directing, Acting, and promoting diversity and excellence onstage. She has taught and directed at universities including UCLA, USC, Cal Poly Pomona, Whittier College, NYU, ACT, Boston University, MIT, the American Shakespeare Center, University of Colorado, and more.

These are extracts from an interview held with Lisa Wolpe on Thursday, 7 August 2014 in Santa Monica, CA.

[TP] = Terri Power [LW] = Lisa Wolpe

TP: You started the Los Angeles Women's Shakespeare Company over 20 years ago. What compelled you to found an all-female company at the time?

LW: Twenty years ago there were a lot fewer powerful roles for women available; it was mostly victim, girlfriend, whore and mother. It was a time when I needed big strong roles to play for the kind of work I wanted to do and I loved Shakespeare. I loved Sam Shepard too, but I was already directing and acting in Shakespeare and classical work, and I just loved the poetry. As an actress I had done a few Moliere and style plays, I had already played Viola and Rosalind, and had experimented in class with cross-gender roles like Malvolio which I loved, and I played *Lear* in small production of an all-female *Lear* here (Los Angeles) when I was only 32. I came in as the understudy to the King of France, and I came in as the understudy to the King of France, and worked my way up through the ranks as actors dropped out for television roles and commercials — four weeks later I was playing *Lear*. Carpe Diem! What a great role! But I love the language, and I just love playing these great characters.

I had a lot of actor training starting with a decade in NYC and at Shakespeare & Company in Lenox, MA. From the time I got interested in theater in college at UC San Diego I was constantly in class, working on subtle performance training through voice, and clown, and combat... my colleagues were smart, strong women looking for meaningful work in the theater, and maybe we didn't fit so easily into the game as it existed then. What I find now is that the game has changed. We are all now great teachers and directors and actors making our own new work, and most of us still working with one another in many ways. Many of my master teachers have helped me with my company, the Los Angeles Women's Shakespeare Company over the past 20 years – Natsuko Ohama, Merry Conway, Tina Packer, Kristin Linklater – so many brilliant women working together who made an indelible mark with 20 years of all-female, multi-cultural Shakespeare. I'm very proud of having founded LAWSC and to have been a Producing Artistic Director of such a fine company all of these years. It has allowed me to "be the change I wanted to see", as they say.

I always wanted to make a jewel box for the most talented women I knew, and I've done that, but now I think creating this great work without a serious budget is too hard. There was one year where all the leading men were pregnant, and fifteen years after that everyone's kid had ballet or martial arts or needed braces and it was tougher to get the same women to rehearsal because they were busy and everyone had to prioritize and keep the money flowing in. We have all been working for free for decades, and we can't keep it going that way.

TP: Especially as you get older, when you have paid your dues and now you have a family to support.

LW: Yes, it's madness to deal with the poverty of theater, but there is a huge payoff, which has nothing to do with material things. The upside to that is that I played Richard III twice, I played Iago twice, I played Hamlet twice, and it's been a wonderful, expansive body of work that made its mark on our community. We no longer find Los Angeles to be the misogynistic, racially stereotyped casting pool it once was. There are a lot of women who are producers who have led the field in theater and in film and TV here, it's a very cutting-edge, savvy entertainment community here on the west coast. I'm so glad to be a part of it. I only wish I was better at raising money, so I could really fund this work properly.

LAWSC has created a beautiful legacy, sending a message that women are wonderful in both the female and male roles. As an actor I've played many wonderful female characters, but my most rewarding on-stage experiences have been portraying some of the greatest male roles ever written within my own all-female company — *Hamlet, Richard III, Angelo, Romeo, Iago, Shylock* — brilliant, complex characters. One of the reasons as to why I founded the company was to create bigger parts for women.

Gender bending is, of course, written into the Shakespeare plays, which were originally performed by all-male companies. The male roles in Shakespeare are written in the perfect style for brilliant investigations of personal identity, which of course includes an exploration of gender expectations and offer self-reflective philosophical flights of genius in the face of societal pressure. There's a titillating level of gender play written into the plays, language which we all recognize was originally written more or less exclusively for the men to play with, but there's something very exciting now in that a wider variety of artists are being allowed the abundant feast of language which the male roles afford.

Over the last ten years I have worked more with men playing the female roles, and recently I have met and worked with increasing numbers of non-cisgender and trans actors who are entering the work place. There's a huge grassroots movement to empower a more inclusive and diverse casting pool to be at center of the new theatre scene.

New concepts are offering more and more ways to reinterpret the plays, and include a greater range of humanity in casting them. In London I recently brought together forty artists with the help of the Young Vic and King's College. Our multicultural ensemble of actors featured gay, straight, male, female, and trans artists working on Shakespeare scenes together, experimenting with various permutations of cross-gender casting and putting people of color into leading male parts.

Many people are working to increase racial diversity and gender parity onstage. And beyond the work being done with Shakespeare, there are more and more new female playwrights taking the stage, more people of color are writing and getting produced, more gender-queer producers and makers of new and devised work around identity and representation are, I think, presenting new stories that are very exciting to contemporary audiences. I just directed a completely gender-flipped production of Thomas Middleton's *The Revengers* at UCLA, where non-white actors made up most of the cast. Women played the rapists and men played the female victims of rape in a play wherein few of those female rape victims were even afforded personal names by the playwright, let alone interesting texts to speak onstage. The production was a thrilling one that inspired much conversation and was a very relevant exploration of a "problem play".

Now, we see that women are playing male roles like *Hamlet* and *Iago* on stages all over the world, while men are now once again working to portray *Ophelia* and *Desdemona*. Some productions are "cross-gendering" (a woman playing *Hamlet* as male) some are "re-gendering" (the *Duke* becomes a *Duchess*) and some are experimenting with asexuality or trans gender or gender queer characterizations, which cannot render placements on a heteronormative masculine/feminine binary.

TP: That is excellent.

LW: Yes, but it doesn't happen without people being activists. We are grateful for The Kilroys List[2] and for all producers that hire other than non cis-gender white male artists for their theaters.

TP: You worked with the Company of Women and from my records they seemed like they were the first (all-female US Shakespeare company), but I don't know if that's a true analysis of the research. There might be some companies missing from the records.

LW: I worked with Kristin Linklater for quite awhile – I first started training with her when I was 19 – and five years later I joined her

Company of Women which was an international all-female company. I played *Henry V* is our inaugural production. It was a wonderful training ground, Kristin partnered with Harvard psychologist Dr. Carol Gilligan, and for a few years we did a lot of writing and a lot of experimentation as performers. We would do residencies at various universities and bring the actors together with the university women who were professors and grad students to explore cross-gendering Shakespeare, working along with groups of young girls from the community, exploring personhood and literacy and rituals. We would all do clown and stage combat and voice and Shakespeare together. It was a very fruitful time for me to be working on male roles in such a powerful international multicultural group of women. We all had our teaching skills, and we were all performers. Carol had pioneered a great deal of work in child psychology that had to do with the experience of growing up in girls instead of boys = she would write about how a young girl's house is wallpapered with lies, and that one in three women has been raped, and that there are no strong role models for women, and we stepped onstage with a purpose. The Company of Women didn't find the funding it needed to continue to grow, and I had left the group just before it's second and final production, which was an all-female *King Lear*, but it was a wonderful exploratorium while it lasted.

TP: Yes, but I feel that there has been a big feminist move from the 80s when there were a lot more women doing progressive work and moving forward. Then we had this weird 1950s-ification of women and we went back to a culture where women are doing pole dancing, and we want to be like the women on 'Mad Men' and a throwback to the 1950s, such as *Desperate Housewives*; there was an emphasis on being a 'housewife' as an ideal.

LW: Yes, that's right. There's always a backlash. There's a big backlash now about what is feminism and who needs it. So it's not over. You can see it clearly when you look at funding for women's work in the theater, and how hard it is to get significant money into what are still not considered mainstream productions. Productions in which women's typical identity profiles are not sold as "Desperate Housewives".

Feminism is important because things have been so unbalanced for so long but of all the "isms", humanism is, I hope, I word we can unite behind. The gender boxes of "behavior expectation" are not what they once were. We should never have excluded women in the first place, and didn't always.

TP: There seems to be a renewed interest in our culture to explore the works of Shakespeare through the lens of gender in a variety of approaches. Why do you think that is?

LW: Recently I've been touring my solo show, "Shakespeare and the Alchemy of Gender" through the US and Canada and the U.K. It's a piece in which I play both male and female characters and explore identity through cross-gender Shakespearean performance. I use fragments of the many roles I have played, from *Hamlet* to *Shylock*, to explore violence and forgiveness, tyranny and resilience, and build empathy and compassion through the context of cross-gender performance. Young people still love Shakespeare, I can tell you that! And that seems to be true all over the world.

I recently directed a production of "The Winter's Tale" which was the first all-female multicultural Shakespeare that Canada's ever seen. In the week we opened, the big newspaper there which is called the *Globe and Mail* called it one of the top five arts events that was a 'must see' in Canada, and the other four were not theatre pieces. This is for a very small production with less than a hundred seats. What's trending in Canada now was trending in LA twenty years ago, and gender bending is trending now. Everything I ever thought about all-female Shakespeare is still true. It's sexy, it's smart, it's powerful, it's challenging. It will never be boring. It's never been boring, it's never going to be boring. It's like surfing — the waves always seem to be different, but surfers have the best smiles in the world. Surfing with words and shifting oneself fluidly along the spectrum of identity finds its athleticism and style in the way that you catch the turn of the phrase. It always helps, as you say, to know more and more about the play, because you're never quite done polishing wordplay and gender play and all kinds of skills required for advanced performance. The personal lens is increasingly prismatic.

TP: Yes, I think it's that thing about great art; we come to it with our own context and then we see it different. The audience is always different too. As an actor you might explore [ideas] in rehearsal but the minute an audience enters, and it's a different audience every night, it just completely changes. It breathes.

LW: Completely.

TP: The performance breathes. Which it can't do in film. This is one of the aspects of theatre that is so different from film; that it is so alive and breathing with an audience.

LW: I agree with you.

TP: Is gender crossing difficult?

LW: For the men playing women to find they are afforded less space, fewer words, to feel what it's like to be undressed with someone's eyes; to be rejected and find your survival can depend upon whether you please others, it can be very difficult and also eye-opening. Women in male roles can and must walk with empowerment, with authority, and explore and own being direct and clear and in charge of the scene. For some people it's easy, for some it doesn't seem possible. Some are really attached to their gender identity, or find it easy to play a position on a gender spectrum that refers to an old-school gender binary of masculine/feminine.

I get so much benefit out of playing a guy who is as interesting as *Hamlet*; the gender question is only a part of the work. The mapping of the mind and the soul, the political arena, the parsing out of how it is subtly different to play *Hamlet* than any other being. I think a lot of the expertise involved in playing male roles has to do with physical acting and vocal choices; how do you center your body for one thing. It's not simple to drop your body center to your inner thigh from your face. Women almost always gesture from the face or from the heart, and gesturally, space is often taken and then given up in a constant dance of deflection and apology. Some of that seems stereotypical, but its an interesting place to start, with a basic examination of what we bring to the role, and what the story demands.

There are lots of choices you have to make as a leading man, interesting philosophical moments, questions of survival, about what might you regret, and what will you consider honorable. You struggle with being expected to have children when you don't want children, or to marry when you don't want to marry, or to kill someone when you don't want to kill someone; the actor works to link the character to an internal authenticity while on the outside portraying expertly what you intend to seem to be. It's a great opportunity to explore a wider conversation around identity and responsibility.

Now, when a more diverse group of people on the planet are walking in each other's shoes, our audiences can sit in wonder at the way we see each other – or make each other invisible. We find great numbers of artists now exploring race and gender onstage. We live in a world of Shakespearean experimentalists presenting new levels of excellence onstage every day, and I am proud to be paddling out on this new wave of thinkers and players.

Notes

Introduction

1. The reader may wish to review Orgel (1996: xiv–4).
2. Reference found in *Playbill* – 16 November 1999.
3. Claire Dowie is a solo performance artist based in the UK that began in stand-up theatre and now specialises in queer performances of gender. She writes her own works that are usually quite political and transformative. Her production of *H to He (I'm Turning Into a Man)* has been toured throughout the UK for several years and was performed at Bath Spa University on 13 October 2008 in the University Theatre and presented by Bath Spa Live. Whilst visiting Bath Spa University, Dowie held an open workshop for my students enrolled on my Staging Shakespeare module. I also conducted an informal interview with Dowie at this time and later secured a formal interview with the artist in July 2009. The quotes from Dowie in this section are from the 2008 workshop.
4. See *The Second Sex* by Simone De Beauvoir, New York: Vintage Books New Edition, 1997.
5. See *Female Impersonation* by Carole-Ann Tyler, New York: Routledge, 2003.

1   Gender Theory

1. I use the term 'beingness' in relation to a state of conscious 'being' borrowing from Jean-Paul Sartre's *Being and Nothingness* published in French in 1943 and in English in 1956.
2. See 'Doing Gender, Determining Gender: Transgender People, Gender Panics, and the Maintenance of the Sex/Gender/ Sexuality System' by Westbrook and Schilt, in Gender and Society, February 2014, 28(1), 32–57.
3. See Foucault 2000. Truth and Power, pp. 111–133 in Paul Rabinow, series ed. *Essential Works of Foucault 1954–1984*. New York: The New Press. Vol. 3, *Power*, J.B. Faubion, ed.
4. See childhood research studies conducted on the effects of gender-typed toys by Jeffrey Trawick-Smith and Judith Elaine Blakemore 'Gender Development' 2008 Psychology Press.

2   Actor–Audience Dynamics at Play in Gender Performance

1. My use of this term is in reference to Eugenio Barba's use of 'Extra-Daily' performance.

3   ShakesQueer

1. The reader may wish to read Halberstam's *The Drag King Book, Female Masculinity, and In a Queer Time and Place: Transgender Bodies, Subcultural Lives.*
2. FTM refers to a female to male transsexual. An FTM transgender or transsexual is a person born biologically female who transitions to become male either through gender appropriation or through medical intervention.

4   Case Study – All-Female Julius Caesar

1. Taken from the Jenni Murray 6 December 2012 BBC Radio Four interview with Phyllida Lloyd.
2. Taken from the Julius Caesar Donmar production 'Behind the Scenes Guide' written by Hannah Price and edited by Sam Maynard.

5   Opportunity in Performing Shakespeare is a Drag for Women

1. British Black and Asian Shakespeare Symposium held at July 2013 at the University of Warwick.
2. Figures taken from 'Discrimination and the Female Playwright' by Sheri Wilner and Julia Jordan. GIA, 21(1) (Spring 2010) 2009 Conference Proceedings.
3. In a personal interview, I sat down with Joanne Zipay, director and founder of the Judith Shakespeare Company, in NYC 12 November 2005. For research I interviewed Zipay on a number of topics including the inspiration for starting her company, the future of women playing men in performance and the pitfalls associated with producing theatre with all-female productions.
4. The use of the description of cross-casting women in male Shakespeare roles can be found in many publicity documents, scholarly writings and theatrical reviews, including SGT 'experiments' with gender circa 2002–4.
5. From the original *Daily Telegraph* review of the production by Charles Spencer in Elizabeth Klett's '"O, How This Mother Swells Up Toward My Heart": Performing Mother and Father in Helena Kaut-Howson's Cross-Gender King Lear' *Shakespeare Bulletin* 22 September 2005.
6. See Jonas, Susan and Suzanne Bennett, 'Report on the Status of Women: A Limited Engagement', Prepared for the New York State Council on the Arts Theatre Program, January 2002.
7. The reader may wish to review the web resource: http://www.equity.org.uk/ news-and-events/equity-news/equitys-womens-committee-research-into-casting/?preview=true accessed January 14, 2014.
8. This quote was taken from the Equity News website http://www.equity.org .uk/news-and-events/equity-news/equity-calls-on-ace-to-monitor-casting/ accessed January 14, 2014.

6   All-Male Companies

1. Taken from 2003 season campaign document: http://www.graphicthought-facility.com/shakespeares-globe-theatre-2003-season-campaign/ accessed on 9 July 2014.

2. I am referring to the Dame (cross-dressed) characters of the pantomime stage that are very popular in the UK and who have similarities to Drag Queen performances.

7 The Female Players and All-Female Companies

1. See 'Breeches Birth' by Laurence Senelick in *The Changing Room: Sex, Drag and Theatre* (London: Routledge, 2000), 206–223.
2. See the *New York Times* article 'Women in Male Roles: Long List of Prominent Actresses Who Have Yielded To That Ambition', author unknown, published February 12, 1911.
3. The first black performer playing Othello was Ira Aldridge in the nineteenth century and the first black actor to play the role on Broadway was Paul Robeson in 1943. Robeson still holds the record for playing the longest-running Shakespeare role in a Broadway production.
4. There are numerous records of other productions and companies including an all-female company led by Australian Louise Dunn around the1930s and notably Marion Potts directed an all-female *Bell Shakespeare* production of *The Taming of the Shrew* presented at the Sydney Opera House in October, 2009.
5. When I refer to the 'voice', I am referring to the sound, pitch, strength and clarity of an actor's speaking. 'Voicework' is the exercises, applications and practices that give strength, stretch and colour the vocal delivery of an actor's voice.
6. Taken from my personal notes on a question-and-answer session held at the Walker Space on 13 November 2005 between the *Taming of the Shrew* company members and the audience.
7. Taken from my personal interview with Joann Zipay in 2014.
8. From 2014 personal email interview with Sheila Proctor.

8 Creative Casting

1. All quotes taken from Oregon Shakespeare Festival Playbill volume 1 2001. From the Director: Creativity, Spirit, and True Power in *The Tempest* by Penny Metropulos.
2. Known for his highly experimental Opera and Classical theatre productions that sometimes fuse cultural traditions and theatrical styles to create mesmerising pieces of art.

9 Queer Shakespeare

1. From web blog post connected to Victor Fiorillo's article 'Curio Theatre Company Doing Lesbian Romeo and Juliet' in *Philadelphia Magazine's* webpages: http://www.phillymag.com/news/2013/09/12/lesbian-romeo-juliet-curio-theatre-company/ accessed 6 June 2014.
2. The Defense of Marriage Act (DOMA) was a Federally recognised act passed during Bill Clinton's presidency that defined 'marriage' as being between a man and a woman only. DOMA was argued as discriminatory and it was felt that it denied gays and lesbians rights that heterosexual couples enjoyed.

After years of political struggle and court battles, the Supreme Court deemed DOMA unconstitutional on 26 August 2013 paving the way for same-sex marriages to be recognised Federally in the United States.

11 Interview with Lisa Wolpe

1. Wolpe directed the premiere production of *The Winter's Tale* for the all-female Canadian company Classic Chic in 2014.
2. The Kilroys list is an annual list of highly praised new plays written by female-identified artists.
3. Here she is referring to Colorado Shakespeare's 2014 productions of Henry IV parts I and II wherein the role of Westmoreland was played by Vanessa Morosco.
4. Referring to Oregon Shakespeare Festival's artistic director Bill Rauch.

Annotated Reading List

For volumes focusing on *gender in theatrical performance* see Aston (1999), Bulman (2008), Case (1988), Diamond (1988), Dolan (1999), Donkin and Clement (1993), Goodman (1998), Halberstam (1998), Howard (2009), Klett (2009), Lenz, Greene and Neely (1983), Minoru and Shapiro (2006), Orgel (1996), Robertson (1998), Senelick (2000), Troka, Lebesco and Noble (2002), Tyler (2003) and Volcano and Halberstam (1999). For *articles, papers and chapters* see Avila, Elaine (2014), Blair, Rhonda (1993), Derr (2013), Gompertz (2012), Higgins (2012), Hilton (2013), Lublin (2012), Patterson (2010), Placino (2012), Rosenberg (2001), Schechner (2010), Soloski (2013), Wells (2009), Wolper (1996) and Zipay (2005). For studies of *gender in sociological performance*, see Bornstein (1994), Butler (1999), Chedgzoy (1995), Cherney, Vance, Glover Ruane, and Ryalls (2003), Emolu (2014), Feinberg (1996, 1998), Freeman (2007), Halberstam (1998, 2005), Hanna (1991), Lloyd (2013), Montgomery and Stewart (2012), Rahilly (2014), RuPaul (1996), Schilt and Westbrook (2009), Seidler, Victor J. (1989) and Tannen (1990).

For details on *gender programming* there are varying perspective to consider. I recommend reviewing Bornstein (1994), Butler (1999) Cherney, Vance, Glover Ruane, and Ryalls (2003), De Beauvoir (1997), Emolu (2014), Feinberg (1996, 1998), Freeman (2007), Lloyd (2013), Montgomery and Stewart (2012), Rahilly (2014), Schilt and Westbrook (2009) and Seidler (1989). For more information and studies on *transgender performance and theory* see Feinberg (1996, 1998), Halberstam (1998, 2005), Hanna (1991), Lloyd (2013), Rahilly (2014), RuPaul (1996), Schilt and Westbrook (2009), Serano (2013), Troka, Lebesco and Noble (2002) and Volcano and Halberstam (1999).

There are many *feminist theories, practices and approaches* to be studied. In terms of cross-gender performance and the points raised in this volume, I recommend a review of Aston (1995, 1999), Brinklow (2012), Butler (1999), Case (1988), Cochrane (2012), Crow (2000), De Beauvoir (1997), Derr (2013), Diamond (1988), Donkin and Clement (1993), Dworkin (1987), Gompertz (2012), Nestor (2011), Rutter (1988), Schechner (2010), Serano (2013), Taylor (2005), Valian (1999), Wolper (1996) and Zipay (2005). To learn more on the subject and practice of *Queer theatre and performance* see Bernstein (2006), Blair (1993), Bornstein (1994), Donkin and Clement (1993), Donkin Chedgzoy (1995), Halberstam (1998), RuPaul (1996), Senelick (2000), Solomon and Minwalla (2002), Troka, Lebesco and Noble (2002), Tyler (2003) and Volcano and Halberstam (1999).

For studies on *women and Shakespeare* there are a great deal of resources to examine. I am particularly interested in volumes, chapters and articles that have gender performance as a focus and that frame arguments with a feminist viewpoint. I recommend taking a look at Avila (2014), Brinklow (2012), Chedgzoy (1995), Derr (2013), Donkin and Clement (1993), Gompertz (2012), Howard (2009), Klett (2009), Lawton (2014), Lenz, Greene and Neely (1983), Nestor (2011), Placino (2012), Rutter (1988), Schechner (2010), Taylor (2005), Wolper (1996) and

Zipay (2005). Studies and articles on *women in male roles* include Avila (2014), Blair (1993), Bulman (2008), Brinklow (2012), Carson and Karim-Cooper (2008), Derr (2013), Donkin and Clement (1993), Goodman (1998), Halberstam (1998), Hanna (1991), Haun (2013), Henderson (2012), Higgins (2012), Howard (2009), Klett (2005, 2009), Lawton (2014), Nestor (2011), Robertson (1998), Senelick (2000), Soloski (2013), Theodorczuk (2013), Troka, Lebesco and Noble (2002), Turney (2013), Volcano and Halberstam (1999), Wolper (1996) and Zipay (2005).

For selected studies on *cross-dressing in performance* see Beckerman (1962), Bernstein (2006), Bulman (2008), Carson and Karim-Cooper, Eds. (2008), Dolan (1999), Donkin and Clement (1993), Goodman (1998), Halberstam (1998), Howard (2009), Klett (2009), Minoru and Shapiro (2006), Orgel (1996), Robertson (1998), RuPaul (1996), Senelick (2000), Troka, Lebesco and Noble (2002), Tyler (2003) and Volcano and Halberstam (1999).For a general overview of *Shakespeare's theatre and original conditions of performance* see Beckerman (1962), Gurr (2004), Kinney (2003), Lublin (2012), Orgel (1996), Rosenberg (2001), Schoone-Jongen (2008), Southworth (2000) and Thomson (1992, 1999). For studies and articles covering aspects of *men in female roles* see Beckerman (1962), Bernstein (2006), Bulman (2008), Carson and Karim-Cooper (2008), Dolan (1999), Feinberg (1996), Goodman (1998), Hilton (2013), Lublin (2012), Minoru and Shapiro (2006), Orgel (1996), Patterson (2010), Rosenberg (2001), RuPaul (1996), Rylance (2003), Schoone-Jongen (2008), Senelick (2000), Solomon and Minwalla (2002), Thomson (1992), Tyler (2003) and Wells (2009). For studies and articles on Shakespeare's *boy players* see Beckerman (1962), Lublin (2012), Minoru and Shapiro (2006), Orgel (1996), Patterson (2010), Rosenberg (2001), Schoone-Jongen (2008), Senelick (2000), Thomson (1992) and Wells (2009).

For an emphasis on *Japanese theatrical performance and gender* see Brandon (1998), Fraleigh and Nakamura (2006), Minoru and Shapiro (2006), Oida and Marshall (1997), Robertson (1998), Senelick (2000) and Suzuki (1986, 2002). Special *empirical studies on gender representation* in theatre and the arts include Dean (2008), Glassberg Sands, (2009) and Silverstein (2014).

To examine articles covering *specific productions and companies* that are not wholly reviews see the following: Shakespeare's Globe Theatre productions of *Twelfth Night* directed by Tim Carroll, Bulman (2008), Carson and Karim-Cooper, Eds. (2008), Hilton (2013), Rylance (2003) and Silverstone (2005). For reviews and materials on Lloyd's *Julius Caesar* see Cochrane (2012), Gompertz (2012), Haun (2013), Henderson (2012), Higgins (2012), Murray (2012), Peacock (2012), Rojas (2012), Soloski (2013), Theodorczuk (2013), Turney (2013) and Williams (2012). For details on Curio Theatre Company's *Romeo and Juliet* take a look at Koza (2013), and for selected articles on the Oregon Shakespeare Festival and their productions see Kendt (2006) and Lawton (2014).

Reading List

All citations from Shakespeare, unless otherwise indicated, are taken from the Arden edition (1998, London: Bloomsbury Arden Shakespeare).

Anon (1911) *'Women in Male Roles: Long List of Prominent Actresses Who Have Yielded To That Ambition'*, New York Times, 12 February.

Aston, Elaine (1995) *An Introduction to Feminism and Theatre,* London: Routledge.

Aston, Elaine (1999) *Feminist Theatre Practice: A Handbook,* London: Routledge.

Avila, Elaine (2014) 'Lisa Wolpe Uses Shakespeare to Bend Gender Roles', *American Theatre,* 13 August 2014.

Barry, Peter (1995) *Beginning Theory: An Introduction to Literary and Cultural Theory,* Manchester: Manchester University Press, 121.

Bean, John C. (1983) 'Comic Structure and the Humanizing of Kate in *The Taming of the Shrew'*, in *The Women's Part,* Swift Lenz, Gayle Greene, and Carol Thomas Neely, Eds., Chicago: University of Illinois Press, Urbana and Chicago, Illini Books edition.

Beckerman, Bernard (1962) *Shakespeare at the Globe 1599–1609,* New York: The Macmillan Company.

Bernstein, Robin (2006) *Cast Out: Queer Lives in Theatre,* Ann Arbor, MI: University of Michigan Press, 2006.

Blair, Rhonda (1993) 'Not … But/Not-Not-Me: Musings on Cross-Gender Performance', in *Upstaging Big Daddy,* Ellen Donkin and Susan Clement, Eds., Ann Arbor, MI: The University of Michigan Press.

Bloom, Harold (1998) *Shakespeare: The Invention of the Human,* New York: Riverhead Books.

Bogart, Anne (2001) *A Director Prepares,* London: Routledge.

Bornstein, Kate (1994) *Gender Outlaw: On Men, Women and the Rest of Us,* New York: Routledge.

Brandon, James R. (1998) 'Zeami on Acting: Values for the Western Actor', in *Zeami and the No Theatre in the World,* Benito Ortolani and Samuel L. Leiter, Eds., New York: CASTA.

Brecht, Bertolt (1964) *Brecht on Theatre: 1933–1947,* New York: Hill and Wang.

Brett, Phillip, Elizabeth Wood, and Gary C. Thomas, Eds. (1994) *Queering the Pitch,* New York: Routledge.

Brinklow, Adam L. (2012) 'Woman's Will Shakes Up Shakespeare', *Curve Magazine,* 20 June.

Bulman, J. C., Ed. (2008) *Shakespeare Re-Dressed: Cross-Gender Casting in Contemporary Performance,* Cranbury: Rosemount Publishing and Printing Corp.

Butler, Judith (1999) *Gender Trouble,* New York: Routledge.

Carson, Christie and Farah Karim-Cooper, Eds. (2008) *Shakespeare's Globe: A Theatrical Experiment,* London: Cambridge University Press.

Case, Sue-Ellen (1988) *Feminism and Theatre,* London: Macmillan Publishers.

Chambers, Colin (2004) *Inside the Royal Shakespeare Company,* London: Routledge.

Chedgzoy, Kate (1995) *Shakespeare's Queer Children: Sexual Politics and Contemporary Culture*, Manchester: Manchester University Press.

Cherney, Isabelle D., Kelly-Vance, Lisa, Glover, Katrina Gill, Ruane, Amy, Ryalls, Brigette Oliver (2003) 'The Effects of Stereotyped Toys and Gender on Play Assessment in Children Aged 18–47 Months', *Educational Psychology*, 23(1), 95–106.

Clapp, Susannah (2014) 'Maxine Peake is a Delicately Ferocious Prince of Denmark', *The Observer*, 20 September.

Cochrane, Kira (2012) 'Phyllida Lloyd: How to Humanise Margaret Thatcher', *The Guardian*, 5 January.

Crow, Barbara A. (2000) *Radical Feminism: A Documentary Reader*, New York: New York University Press.

Dean, Debra (2008) 'Changing Gender Portrayal: Promoting Employment Opportunities for Women in the Performing Arts', *Age Gender and Performer Employment in Europe*. Report on Research for the International Federation of Actors (FIA) Project.

De Beauvoir, Simone (1997) *The Second Sex*, trans. Parshley H.M. Ed., New York: Vintage Classics, New Edition.

Derr, Holly L. (2013) 'All-Woman Shakespeare: A Dying Tradition?' *Ms Magazine Blog*, 27 August.

Diamond, Elin (1988) 'Brechtian Theory/Feminist Theory: Towards a Gestic Feminist Criticism', *The Drama Review*, 32.

Dolan, Jill (1999) *Presence and Desire: Essays on Gender, Sexuality, Performance*, Ann Arbor, MI: Michigan University Press.

Donkin, Ellen and Susan Clement (1993) *Upstaging Big Daddy*, Ann Arbor, MI: University of Michigan Press.

Dworkin, Andrea (1987) *Intercourse*, New York: Free Press.

Emolu, Esra (2014) 'Play, Toys and Gender Socialization', *Journal Plus Education*, XI(2), 22–30.

Feinberg, Leslie (1996) *Transgender Warriors: Making History from Joan of Arc to Dennis Rodman*, Boston, MA: Beacon Press.

Feinberg, Leslie (1998) *Trans Liberation: Beyond Pink or Blue*, Boston, MA: Beacon Press.

Fischlin, Daniel and Mark Fortier, Eds. (2000) *Adaptations of Shakespeare: A Critical Anthology of Plays from the 17th Century to the Present*, Oxon: Routledge.

Fraleigh, Sondra and Tamah Nakamura (2006) *Hijikata Tatsumi and Ohno Kazuo*, Oxon: Routledge.

Freeman, Nancy K. (2007) 'Preschoolers' Perceptions of Gender-Appropriate Toys and Their Parents' Beliefs about Genderized Behaviors: Miscommunication, Mixed Messages, or Hidden Truth?' *Early Childhood Education Journal*, 34(5), 357–366.

Fujita, Minoru and Michael Shapiro (2006) *Transvestism and the Onnagata Traditions in Shakespeare and Kabuki*, Kent: Global Oriental.

Gilreath, Shannon (2006) *Sexual Politics: The Gay Person in America Today*, Akron, OH: University of Akron Press.

Glassberg Sands, Emily (2009) 'Opening the Curtain on Playwright Gender: An Integrated Economic Analysis of Discrimination in American Theatre', Princeton University, 15 April. Princeton University Senior Theses, can be accessed at: http://arks.princeton.edu/ark:/88435/dsp01rr171z100

Goodman, Liz (1998) *The Routledge Reader in Gender and Performance*, London: Routledge.

Gompertz, Will (2012) 'Director Phyllida Lloyd: We Need More Women in Theatre', *BBC News*, 6 December.

Gurr, Andrew (2004) *Playgoing in Shakespeare's London*, Cambridge: Cambridge University Press.

Halberstam, Judith (1998) *Female Masculinity*, Durham, NC: Duke University Press.

Halberstam, Judith (2005) *In a Queer Time and Place: Transgender Bodies, Subcultural Lives*, New York: New York University Press.

Hanna, Gillian (1991) *Monstrous Regiment: Four Plays and a Collective Celebration*, London: Nick Hern.

Hanna, Judith L. (1988) *Dance, Sex and Gender*, Chicago: University of Chicago Press.

Haun, Harry (2013) 'That Dame in the Cellblock: An All-Female *Julius Caesar* at St. Ann's Warehouse', *New York Observer*, 29 October.

Henderson, Grace (2012) 'Interview with Frances Barber', *Aesthetica Magazine Blog*.

Henderson, Kathy (2013) 'Paul Chahidi on His Gender-Bending Star Turn in Twelfth Night & Exploring New York With His Family', *Broadway.com*, 7 November.

Higgins, Charlotte (2012) 'Can an All-Women *Julius Caesar* Work?', *The Guardian*, 19 November.

Hilton, Als (2013) 'The Mirror Has Two Faces: The Joys and Mysteries of Shakespeare', *The New Yorker*, 25 November.

Howard, Tony (2009) *Women as Hamlet*, Cambridge: Cambridge University Press.

Kendt, Rob (2006) 'Bill Rauch's Oregon Trail', *Theatre Communication Group*, October.

Kinney, Arthur F. (2003) *Shakespeare by Stages: An Historical Introduction*, Oxford: Blackwell Publishing.

Klett, Elizabeth (2009) *Cross-Gender Shakespeare and English National Identity*, New York: Palgrave Macmillan.

Klett, Elizabeth (2005) '"O, How This Mother Swells Up Toward My Heart": Performing Mother and Father in Helena Kaut-Howson's Cross-Gender *King Lear*', *Shakespeare Bulletin*, 22 September.

Koza, Kirsten (2013) 'A Lesbian Version of "Romeo and Juliet" Gets Death Threats', *The Blot Magazine*, 21 October.

Lloyd, Moya (2013) 'Heteronormativity and/as Violence: The "Sexing" of Gwen Araujo', *Hypatia*, 28(4), 818–834.

Lawson, Mark (2014) 'Polonia and the Prince of Denmark: When Theatre Goes Gender-Blind', *New Statesman*, 26 September–2 October, 86.

Lawton, Jacquline E. (2014) 'No Gents of Verona; or, Let's Dude This', *Theatre Communications Group*, http://www.tcgcircle.org/2014/06/no-gents-of-verona-or-lets-dude-this

Lenz, Carolyn, Gayle Greene, and Carol Neely, Eds. (1983) *The Women's Part*, Chicago: University of Illinois Press, Urbana and Chicago, Illini Books edition.

Lublin, Robert I. (2012) 'Anxious Audiences and the Early Modern English Transvestite Theatre', *Alabama Review*, 65(3), 66–73.

McDermott, Kristen (2000) '*The Tempest* Review', *Theatre Journal*, 52(4), December.

McKellen, Ian (2012) 'Ian McKellen: Shakespeare Enjoyed Sex With Men', *Advocate*, 5 January.

Montgomery, Samantha A., and Stewart, Abigail J. (2012) 'Privileged Allies in Lesbian and Gay Rights Activism: Gender, Generation, and Resistance to Heteronormativity', *Journal of Social Issues*, 68(1), 162–177.

Morris, Sylvia (2012) 'Shakespeare For Women: from Henry V to Julius Caesar' *The Shakespeare Blog* [online] Available at: http://theshakespeareblog.com/2012/09/shakespeare-for-women-from-henry-v-to-julius-caesar/

Murray, Jenni (2012) 'Woman's Hour', *BBC Radio Four*, 6 December.

Nestor, Frank (2011) 'It's a Drag for Women', *Backstage*, 6 April.

Oida, Yoshi, and Marshall, Lorna (1997) *The Invisible Actor*, London: Methuen.

Orgel, Stephen (1996) *Impersonations: The Performance of Gender in Shakespeare's England*, Cambridge: Cambridge University Press.

osfashland.org (2012) https://www.osfashland.org/en/productions/plays/very-merry-wives-of-windsor.aspx

Patterson, Ronan (2010) 'Love's Labours Bewildered', *Shakespeare, Women, Theatre*, Pazmany Peter Catholic University, Budapest, Hungary, 17 September.

Peacock, Louisa (2012) 'Mandatory quotas for Shakespeare plays "would lead to incoherence"', *The Telegraph*, 7 December.

Placino, Portia (2012) 'Portia's Casket | Representation of Women | Shakespeare Voices News for December 12', *The Shakespeare Standard*, 11 December.

Price, Hannah (2012) *Julius Caesar: Behind the Scenes,* Donmar Warehouse production book. Edited by Sam Maynard. http://www.donmarwarehouse.com/~/media/Files/Julius%20Caesar%20Behind%20the%20Scenes%20Guide.ashx

Rahilly, Elizabeth P. (2014) 'The Gender Binary Meets the Gender-Variant Child: Parents' Negotiations with Childhood Gender Variance', *Gender and Society*, 23 December.

Rees, Mandy, Ed. (2007) *Voice and Gender*, Cincinnati, OH: Voice and Speech Trainers Association, Inc.

Robertson, Jennifer (1998) *Takarazuka: Sexual Politics and Popular Culture in Modern Japan*, Los Angeles, CA: University of California Press.

Rodenburg, Patsy (2002) *Speaking Shakespeare*, London: Methuen.

Rojas, John-Paul Ford (2012) 'Royal Shakespeare Company "must be forced to employ equal numbers of male and female actors"', *The Telegraph*, 6 December.

Rose, Judith (2008) 'Performing Gender at the Globe: The Technologies of the Cross-Dressed Actor', *Shakespeare Re-dressed: Cross-Gender Casting in Contemporary Performance*, James C. Bulman, Ed., Cranbury, NJ: Rosemount Publishing and Printing Corp, 210–227.

Rosenberg, Marvin (2001) 'The Myth of Shakespeare's Squeaking Boy Actor – or Who Played Cleopatra?', *Shakespeare Bulletin*, 19(2), 5–6, Spring.

RSC (2005) *Two Gentlemen of Verona Study Guide for Teachers*, Stratford-Upon-Avon: RSC Learning.

RuPaul and RuPaul (1996) *Lettin It All Hang Out: An Autobiography*, New York: Hyperion.

Rutter, Carol (1988) *Clamorous Voices: Shakespeare's Women Today*, London: The Women's Press.

Rylance, Mark (2003) 'Unsex Me Here', *The Guardian*.

Schechner, Richard (2010) 'Casting Without Limits', *American Theatre* – Theatre Communication Group, June.

Schiermeister, Jessica (2015) 'The False Issue of "Illegality" of Female Performance', *Shakespeare Standard,* http://theshakespearestandard.com/false-issue-illegality-female-performance

Schilt, Kristen, and Westbrook, Laurel (2009) 'Doing Gender, Doing Heteronormativity: "Gender Normals," Transgender People and the Social Maintenance of Heterosexuality', *Gender and Society,* 23(4), 440–464.

Schoone-Jongen, Terrence G. (2008) *Shakespeare's Companies.* Surrey: Ashgate Publishing Limited.

Seidler, Victor J. (1989) *Rediscovering Masculinity: Reason, Language and Sexuality.* New York: Routledge.

Senelick, Laurence (2000) *The Changing Room: Sex, Drag and Theatre,* London: Routledge.

Serano, Julia (2013) *Excluded: Making Feminist and Queer Movements More Inclusive,* New York: Seal Press.

Silverstein, Melissa (2014) 'Celluloid Ceiling Report: No Progress in 16 Years for Women in Hollywood', *Indiewire,* 14 January.

Silverstone, Catherine (2005) 'Shakespeare Live: Reproducing Shakespeare at the 'New' Globe Theatre', *Textual Practice,* 19(1), 31–50, Spring.

Silverstone, Catherine (2011) Shakespeare, Trauma and Contemporary Performance, New York: Routledge.

Solomon, Alisa, and Minwalla, Framji (2002) *The Queerest Art: Essays on Lesbian and Gay Theatre,* New York: New York University Press, 14.

Soloski, Alexis (2013) 'Once More Into the Breeches: Gender Bending "Julius Caesar" Has All-Female Cast', *New York Times,* 4 October.

Southworth, John (2000) *Shakespeare The Player,* London: Sutton Publishing.

Spencer, Charles (2009) '*The Taming of the Shrew* at the Novello Theatre, Review', *The Telegraph,* 18 February.

Stokes, Erin (2005) Women Directing Women, Cedar Crest College website, http://www2.cedarcrest.edu/academic/eng/lfletcher/measure/WomenDirectingWomenEstokes.htm

Suzuki, Tadashi (1986) *The Way of Acting,* New York: Theatre Communications Group, Inc.

Suzuki, Tadashi (2002) *The Art of Stillness,* London: Methuen.

Tannen, Deborah (1990) *You Just Don't Understand: Women and Men in Conversation,* New York: Ballantine Books.

Taylor, Nancy (2005) *Women Direct Shakespeare in America: Productions from the 1990s,* Cranbury, NJ: Rosemont Publishing and Printing Corp.

Theodorczuk, Tom (2013) 'Donmar Warehouse Takes a Bite Out of the Big Apple', *London Evening Standard,* 16 October.

Thomson, Peter (1992) *Shakespeare's Theatre,* London: Psychology Press.

Thomson, Peter (1999) *Shakespeare's Professional Career,* Cambridge: Canto Press.

Thomson, Peter (2003) *On Actors and Acting,* Exeter: University of Exeter Press.

Troka, D., Lebesco, K., and Noble, J.B. (2002) *The Drag King Anthology,* New York: Harrington Park Press.

Turney, Eleanor (2013) 'Spotlight On: Cush Jumbo', *A Younger Theatre,* 12 July.

Tyler, Carole-Ann (2003) *Female Impersonation,* New York: Routledge.

Valian, Virginia (1999) *Why so Slow?: The Advancement of Women,* New York: MIT Press.

Volcano, Del LaGrace, and Judith "Jack" Halberstam (1999) *The Drag King Book*, London: Serpent's Tail.

Wells, Stanley (2009) 'Boys Should be Girls: Shakespeare's Female Roles and the Boy Players', *New Theatre Quarterly*, 25(02), 172–177, 19 May.

West, Rebecca (1913) 'Mr. Chesterton in Hysterics', *The Clarion*, 14 November.

West and Zimmerman (2009) 'Accounting for Doing Gender', *Gender and Society*, 23(1), 112–122, February.

Williams, Lauren (2012) 'Phyllida Lloyd: The Iron Lady Is Political in a Feminist Way', *The Metro*, 5 January.

Wolper, Andrea (1996) 'Women and Theatre: The Companies They Keep', *Back Stage*, 26 April–2 May.

Zipay, Joanne (2005) 'Acting, Shakespeare and Gender', *The Soul of the American Actor; America's Artists' Newspaper* (Vol. 7 no. 4, winter 2004/2005).

Original Interviews

Garcia, Lydia (2014) Interview with Terri Power. Ashland, Oregon. 14 February.

Lockhart, Dugald (2014) Interview with Terri Power. Bath, England (via Skype). 2 May.

Proctor, Sheila Snow (2014) Email Interview with Terri Power. Bath, England. 21 March.

Wolpe, Lisa (2014) Interview with Terri Power. Santa Monica, California. 7 August.

Zipay, Joanne (2014) Interview with Terri Power. Palm Springs, California (via Skype). 15 January.

Websites

Chickspeare (2014) http://chickspeare.com [accessed on 8 August].

Los Angeles Women's Shakespeare Company (2010) http://www.lawsc.net [accessed on 2 February].

Oregon Shakespeare Company (2014) https://www.osfashland.org/en.aspx [accessed on 14 July].

Queen's Company (2014) http://queenscompany.org [accessed on 8 August].

Women's Will (2010) http://womenswill.org [accessed on 4 February].

Index

Note: Letter 'n' followed by the locators refer to notes.